BIBLE
HISTORY OVERVIEW

NEW TESTAMENT

BIBLE
HISTORY OVERVIEW

NEW TESTAMENT

GARY OLSBY

Dedicated To My Loving Wife, Tamala,
My Sweetheart Forever.

Oh, Lord, Thank You For Bringing
Her Into My Life!

Artwork provided by Keith Poletiek.

Printed and Bound in the
United States of America

International Standard Book Number: 0-89900-443-1

CONTENTS

NEW TESTAMENT — INTRODUCTION

The assumption is that if you're interested in this New Testament "Overview" study, you've already studied the Old Testament "Overview." The Old Testament study clearly explained the philosophy behind the "Overview" studies. If you have not studied from the Old Testament "Overview", please do so before you go any further with this New Testament study.

RESULTS OF NEW TESTAMENT STUDY

In 1985, we kicked off our Old Testament "Overview", with phenomenal results. We followed this up in 1986 with the New Testament "Overview". Our first few months in the New Testament study showed a 13% increase over the 1985 last quarter averages. So, again, our people responded to the strategy behind this program.

ACTUAL QUOTES OF PARTICIPANTS

"For the first time, this study has put the life of Christ in an easy-to-remember order. It has been a review of the material for me, but really makes sense — finally! This is not a 'dry' study - but a 'living, active, informative' study. I can think of the acrostic and it all is in an understandable order."

"It has taught me more in a short time than any class I've been to. I have been reading on a more regular basis due to this class and that has improved my relationship with Christ."

"This class made Easter the most exciting Easter ever."

"The study has been an exciting way of remembering and learning about the life of Christ. The remembering system that has been worked out makes it fun and easy to recall the events of Christ's life. It has been extremely enjoyable."

"Without exception, this is the most effective study I have participated in for information. Total commitment to a faith in Christ will stand over the long haul only if it can be substantiated with knowledge of who Christ is and what He said and did. Other studies and sermons have provided isolated facts but this is the first *complete presentation* of the *information* regarding our Lord that I have been involved in."

SUNDAY SCHOOL IS FOR

L

I

F

E

IN THE SPIRIT!

- -

What are your expectations for this class?

What can you do to make sure that these expectations are met?

THE FLOW OF BIBLE HISTORY

remember: "beep slowly, jake carries cocoa"

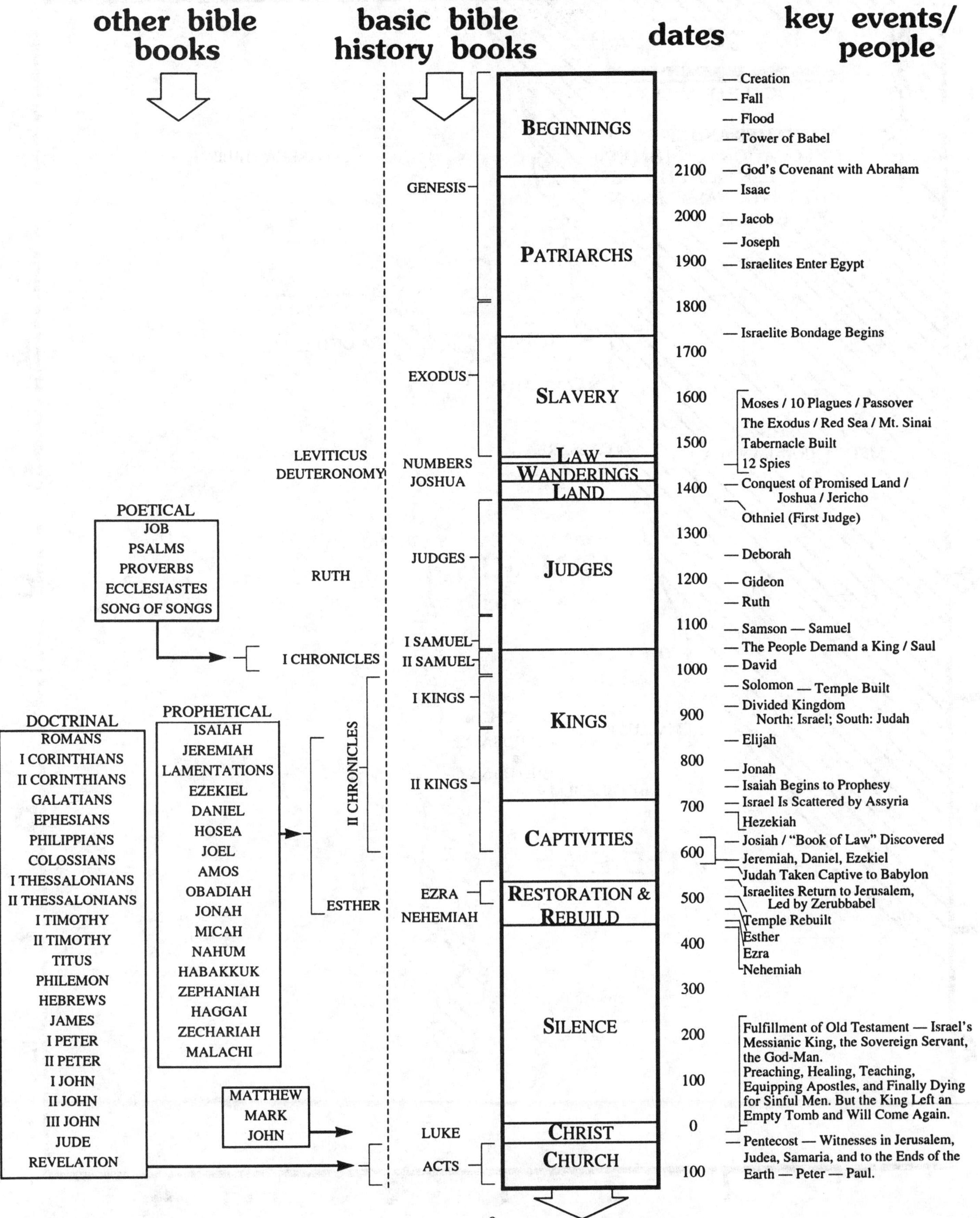

other bible books
basic bible history books
dates
key events/ people
BEGINNINGS
PATRIARCHS
SLAVERY
LAW
WANDERINGS
LAND
JUDGES
KINGS
CAPTIVITIES
RESTORATION & REBUILD
SILENCE
CHRIST
CHURCH
GENESIS
EXODUS
LEVITICUS
DEUTERONOMY
NUMBERS
JOSHUA
POETICAL
JOB
PSALMS
PROVERBS
ECCLESIASTES
SONG OF SONGS
RUTH
JUDGES
I SAMUEL
II SAMUEL
I CHRONICLES
I KINGS
II KINGS
II CHRONICLES
DOCTRINAL
ROMANS
I CORINTHIANS
II CORINTHIANS
GALATIANS
EPHESIANS
PHILIPPIANS
COLOSSIANS
I THESSALONIANS
II THESSALONIANS
I TIMOTHY
II TIMOTHY
TITUS
PHILEMON
HEBREWS
JAMES
I PETER
II PETER
I JOHN
II JOHN
III JOHN
JUDE
REVELATION
PROPHETICAL
ISAIAH
JEREMIAH
LAMENTATIONS
EZEKIEL
DANIEL
HOSEA
JOEL
AMOS
OBADIAH
JONAH
MICAH
NAHUM
HABAKKUK
ZEPHANIAH
HAGGAI
ZECHARIAH
MALACHI
ESTHER
EZRA
NEHEMIAH
MATTHEW
MARK
JOHN
LUKE
ACTS
2100
2000
1900
1800
1700
1600
1500
1400
1300
1200
1100
1000
900
800
700
600
500
400
300
200
100
0
100
— Creation
— Fall
— Flood
— Tower of Babel
— God's Covenant with Abraham
— Isaac
— Jacob
— Joseph
— Israelites Enter Egypt
— Israelite Bondage Begins
Moses / 10 Plagues / Passover
The Exodus / Red Sea / Mt. Sinai
Tabernacle Built
12 Spies
— Conquest of Promised Land / Joshua / Jericho
Othniel (First Judge)
— Deborah
— Gideon
— Ruth
— Samson — Samuel
— The People Demand a King / Saul
— David
— Solomon — Temple Built
— Divided Kingdom North: Israel; South: Judah
— Elijah
— Jonah
— Isaiah Begins to Prophesy
— Israel Is Scattered by Assyria
Hezekiah
— Josiah / "Book of Law" Discovered
— Jeremiah, Daniel, Ezekiel
Judah Taken Captive to Babylon
Israelites Return to Jerusalem, Led by Zerubbabel
Temple Rebuilt
Esther
Ezra
Nehemiah
Fulfillment of Old Testament — Israel's Messianic King, the Sovereign Servant, the God-Man. Preaching, Healing, Teaching, Equipping Apostles, and Finally Dying for Sinful Men. But the King Left an Empty Tomb and Will Come Again.
— Pentecost — Witnesses in Jerusalem, Judea, Samaria, and to the Ends of the Earth — Peter — Paul.

LIFE OF CHRIST MAP

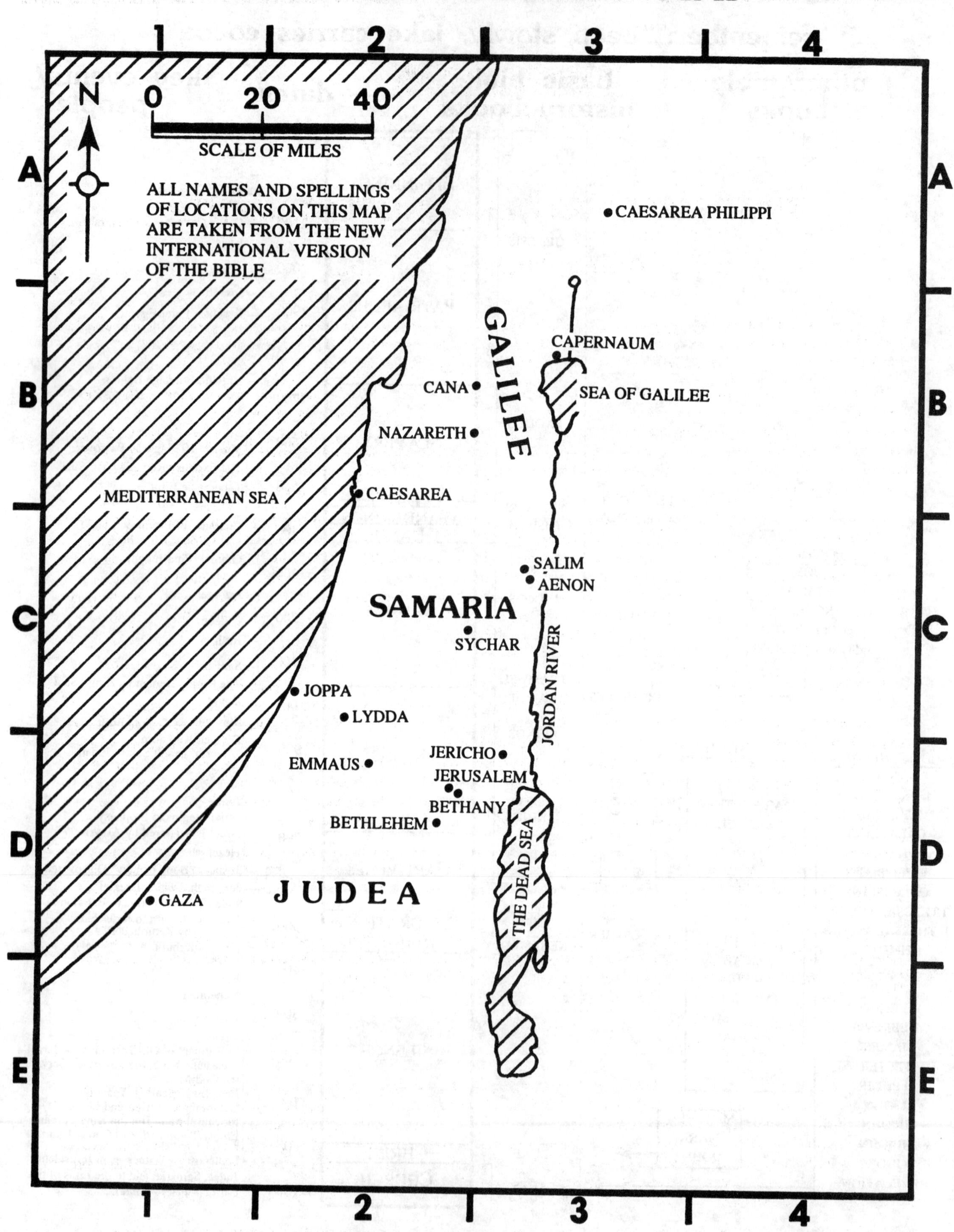

1
2
3
4
A
B
C
D
E
N
0
20
40
SCALE OF MILES
ALL NAMES AND SPELLINGS OF LOCATIONS ON THIS MAP ARE TAKEN FROM THE NEW INTERNATIONAL VERSION OF THE BIBLE
CAESAREA PHILIPPI
GALILEE
CAPERNAUM
CANA
SEA OF GALILEE
NAZARETH
CAESAREA
MEDITERRANEAN SEA
SALIM
AENON
SAMARIA
SYCHAR
JORDAN RIVER
JOPPA
LYDDA
JERICHO
EMMAUS
JERUSALEM
BETHANY
BETHLEHEM
THE DEAD SEA
JUDEA
GAZA

THE PERIOD BETWEEN THE TESTAMENTS

GOD IS STILL IN CONTROL!

From the last Old Testament history book, Nehemiah, to the beginning of New Testament times there was a period of four hundred years. During this time God did not reveal Himself personally to mankind (see Amos 8:11). Therefore it is called the "Period of Silence." As we study the "Life of Christ" it is important that we understand the historical events of this period.

The Persian Empire that we find in power at the close of the Old Testament began to disintegrate. This disintegration was brought about mainly by *Alexander The Great* (336 to 323 B.C.). It was his dream to see a one world Greek empire which would be held together not only by government, but also by the ties of language, customs, and religion. So . . . he set out to conquer the world. One by one the nations fell before him; armies such as Persia, Phoenicia, and Egypt were all defeated by him. He established Greek cultural centers as he went. The Greek way of life was adopted by people everywhere. From his day on through the New Testament period, Greek was the common language of the Mediterranean world, a fact that greatly aided the spread of Christianity.

At Alexander's death, his empire was divided among his generals. For some time (323-198 B.C.). the *Ptolemaic Dynasty in Egypt* ruled over Palestine. Next the *Seleucid Dynasty in Syria* ruled the land of the Jews (198-143). It was during this time, about 285 B.C., that the Old Testament was translated into Greek. This version of the Scriptures is called the "Septuagint," meaning seventy, because seventy noted Hebrew scholars did this great work. You will find it referred to by Roman numerals LXX. During most of this time the Jews had great freedom to do as they pleased. But when Antiochus IV Epiphanes took the throne (175 B.C.) and attempted to subjugate the Jews into a completely Greek society, the Jews revolted and finally in 143 B.C. gained complete independence. This was called the *Maccabean Revolt*, which was followed by the Jewish *Hasmonean Dynasty* (135-63 B.C.)

The Hasmonean Dynasty of the Jews was characterized by a constant struggle for power. Part of the problem was the disagreements between the Pharisees and Sadducees. The *Sadducees* were more interested in politics than they were in religion, though they are considered a religious party. They always associated with the aristocrats and ruling classes. They accepted only the Pentateuch as inspired, resisted oral tradition, and did not believe in angels or the resurrection. They opposed Jesus primarily because they feared that his popularity with the common people would result in trouble with Rome. On the other hand, the *Pharisees* derived their name from a term that means "separated ones". They were very careful about observance of all Jewish laws. They were very much in sympathy with oral tradition, feeling that it was necessary to help the people obey the law. They upheld the very strictest form of Jewish worship. They believed in the resurrection, in punishment and rewards in the afterlife, in angels, in the supremacy of the Pentateuch, and in divine sovereignty over history. They were a religious party, but they were not above "mixing in politics."

A new world power asserted itself in the Mediterranean world in the second century B.C. — *Rome.* In 63 B.C. Pompey captured Jerusalem for Rome. Although the Jews basically ran the country, they did it under Roman rule for years. Many years of struggle and confusion pass by until finally *Herod the Great* was made king of the region in 37 B.C. It was this Herod who was king when Christ was born.

Two characteristics of Roman rule stand out which greatly aided the spread of Christianity; l) law and order, and 2) a civilized system of roads. The combination of these two characteristics made travel for later Christian missionaries relatively safe and peaceful. It should also be said that the neutral attitude of Rome towards Christianity also aided its spread.

IN SUMMARY

Between the time when the last Old Testament book was written and the first New Testament writer took up his pen, some tremendous changes had taken place. The Persian Empire had fallen and a Roman emperor was issuing a decree to be observed by the world. Nehemiah was no longer governor of the Hebrews of Judea; the Jews were ruled by an Idumean king named Herod. The high priest no longer held absolute authority but a great council, the Sanhedrin, exercised religious and political authority over the people. Israel was no longer a small remnant struggling to restore her ruined city in spite of poverty and surrounding unfriendly nations. Instead, there was a densely-populated country with crowded cities. These cities were inhabited by rich merchants who had economic, social, and political strength in the Roman Empire.

The language of the religious leaders had changed, and the people spoke Aramaic and Greek. Their Scriptures were read in Greek.

The intermarriage problems of Nehemiah's day had been solved by a policy of social exclusiveness. The former doctrinal unity of the Jews had given way to division which manifested itself in varied religious sects. These sects were vying with each other for the loyalty and support of the people. The hope of the coming of a king like the great David and realization of the promises made to Abraham had developed into a Messiah-concept which embodied a multitude of bizarre fantasies. The concepts included a hope that Israel would be restored to its former glory. The Jews' idea of messiah was both political and material in character and seemed to lack spiritual depth.

INTRODUCTION TO THE "LIFE OF CHRIST"

THE STRUCTURE OF THE NEW TESTAMENT

HISTORICAL 5	LETTERS 21	PROPHECY 1
GOSPELS: MATTHEW, MARK, LUKE, JOHN	PAULINE (13): ROMANS, 1 CORINTHIANS, 2 CORINTHIANS, GALATIANS, EPHESIANS, PHILIPPIANS, COLOSSIANS, 1 THESSALONIANS, 2 THESSALONIANS, I TIMOTHY, 2 TIMOTHY, TITUS, PHILEMON	REVELATION
ACTS	GENERAL (8): HEBREWS, JAMES, 1 PETER, 2 PETER, I JOHN, 2 JOHN, 3 JOHN, JUDE	

WHY FOUR GOSPELS?

Gospel means "good news" — the good news concerning the birth, life, death, and resurrection of Jesus Christ. Although there is but one gospel, we are given the gospel story through four separate sources. Why? Wouldn't one gospel record be simpler, clearer, and more easily understood? Well . . . it may be simpler, but it would also only give us one view of Christ's life. You see each gospel writer brings a different viewpoint to Christ's life. By seeing four separate but similar views of Christ, we have a much more well-rounded view of what He was really all about.

The four gospels are not really biographies, since they tell very little of Christ's life except the last three years, and especially the last week. Each writer has recorded what he felt was relevant in accomplishing his purpose for his particular audience.

MATTHEW

KEY WORD: *KING*

Matthew wrote especially for the Jews. Jesus' genealogy, the fulfillment of many Old Testament prophecies, His power and authority, and His title as "Son of David" are all emphasized as His Messianic credentials. Matthew wanted the Jews to know that their

Messiah had truly come.

MARK

KEY WORD: *SERVANT*

Mark is a short, vigorous record (notice the continual use of the word: "immediately") that would appeal to the active Romans. There are few quotations from the Old Testament and more miracles mentioned than other gospels. Romans didn't have the Old Testament background of the Jews and they were more interested in deeds than words. Thus, Mark presents Jesus as the "servant" who came to "give His life a ransom for many."

LUKE

KEY WORD: *MAN*

Luke's view of Jesus was that He was a "perfect Man." This gospel record is more historical in nature than the others. Jesus' genealogy goes back to Adam, the first man. As a Perfect Man, He is seen much in prayer. "Luke" is a literary masterpiece that would appeal to cultured Greeks, like Luke himself.

Matthew, Mark, and Luke are called Synoptic Gospels, from Greek words meaning "seeing together" or "seen together." They are so similar in viewpoint and content that they can be printed in parallel columns and seen together. John, writing long after the others were dead, omitted most of what they gave, and added many of Jesus' conversations. He omits the birth, baptism, temptation, sermon on the mount, all the parables, transfiguration, institution of the Lord's Supper, and the agony in Gethsemane.

JOHN

KEY WORD: *GOD*

John portrays Jesus as the Son of God. Written to all mankind, with the purpose of leading men to Christ. Everything in this gospel shines forth the deity of Jesus. John, written perhaps thirty years after the Synoptics, records more of the deep spiritual teachings of Jesus.

Although we have four separate views of Christ's life, one thing is certain: JESUS CHRIST CAME TO EARTH TO DIE, SO THAT I MIGHT LIVE. This must remain as our focus throughout our entire "Life of Christ" study.

PERIODS IN THE "LIFE OF CHRIST"

DATES OF STUDY	PPOST	MATTHEW	MARK	LUKE	JOHN
2–16	PREPARATION	1:1–4:11	1:1–13	1:1–4:13	1:1–18
3–23	POPULARITY	4:12–11:30	1:14–5:43	4:14–9:6	1:19–5:47
3–2 3–9	OPPOSITION	12:1–25:46	6:1–14:11	9:7–21:38	6:1–12:50
3–16	SUFFERING	26:1–27:66	14:12–15:47	22:1–23:56	13:1–19:42
3–23	TRIUMPH	28:1–20	16:1–20	24:1–53	20:1–21:25

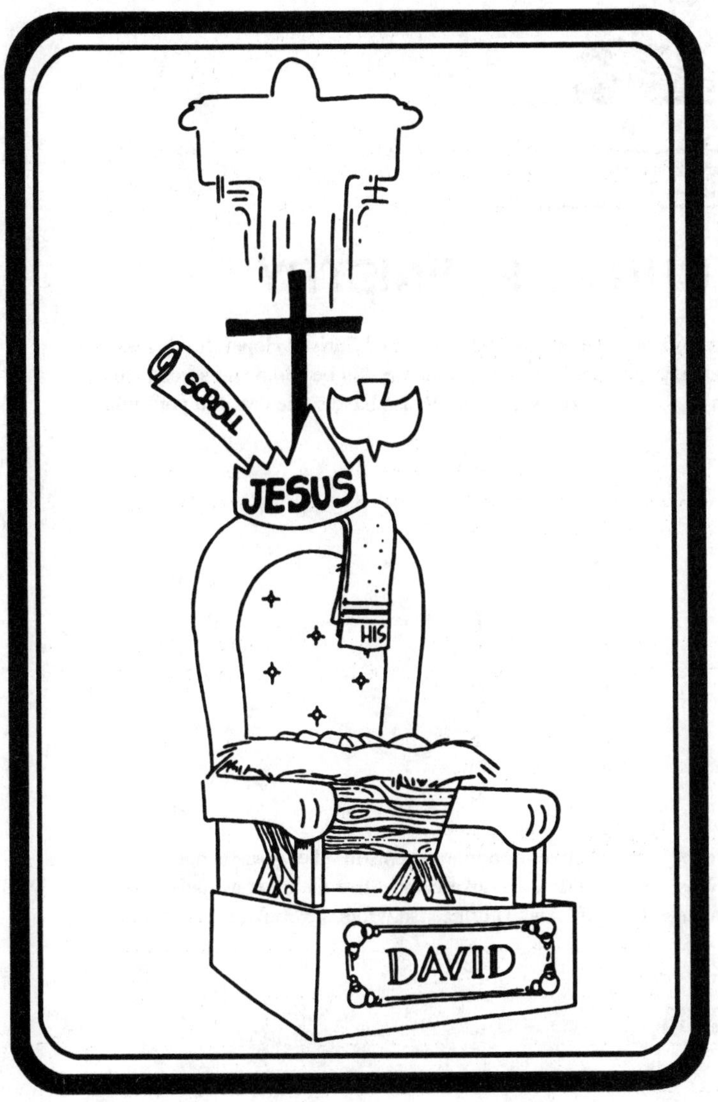

In keeping with our Old Testament "Overview" study, we have a picture for each "basic Bible history" book (see page 9 of New Testament study). Hopefully this picture will help you to remember what we find in the book of Luke.

THE BOOK OF LUKE

Jesus came to sit on the throne of David (manger on throne). He came to serve (towel), fulfill prophecy (scroll), teach (scroll), prepare people for the coming of the Spirit (dove), and to be the King of the Jews (crown). More importantly, He came to die for our sins (cross), to be resurrected from the dead, and to ascend to Heaven to prepare a place for Christians to be with Him forever.

WHO IS JESUS?

DIFFERENT PEOPLE THROUGHOUT HISTORY HAVE SEEN JESUS AS DIFFERENT THINGS

OLD TESTAMENT

— A Star (Num. 24:17,19)
— A Prophet (Deut. 18:15-19)
— A King (Psalm 2:6)
— The Holy One (Psalm 16:10)
— The Anointed One (Psalm 45:7)
— A Priest (Psalm 110:4)
— The Cornerstone (Psalm 115:22)
— The Branch at the Lord (Isaiah 4:2)
— Immanuel (Isaiah 7:13,14)
— A Great Light (Isaiah 9:1,2)
— Counsellor (Isaiah 9:6,7)
— Mighty God (Isaiah 9:6,7)
— Prince of Peace (Isaiah 9:6,7)
— A Shepherd (Isaiah 40:11)
— A Servant (Isaiah 42:1)
— A Lamb (Isaiah 53:7)

NEW TESTAMENT

— Holy One (Mark 1:24)
— Lamb of God (John 1:29)
— Author of Life (Acts 3:15)
— Lord God Almighty (Revelation 15:3)
— Word of Life (I John 1:1)
— Advocate (1 John 2:1)
— The Way (John 14:6)
— Shepherd (1 Peter 2:25)
— Messiah (John 1:41)
— The Truth (John 14:6)
— Saviour (2 Peter 2:20)
— Chief Cornerstone (Ephesians 2:20)
— King of Kings (Revelation 19:16)
— Righteous Judge (2 Timothy 4:8)
— Light of the World (John 5:12)
— Resurrection and Life (John 11:25)

WHO IS JESUS — TO ME?

PREPARATION FOR CHRIST'S MINISTRY

On page 14 you were introduced to the "Post" acrostic, which gives us the five periods in the "Life of Christ." Hopefully this will help you to remember the flow of events in the life of Christ. As we study each one of these periods we will be adding an acrostic to each one, to give it more detail. So . . . you'll not only know the five periods of Christ's life, you'll also have some detail in your mind concerning each one.

Our acrostic for the period of "Preparation" is:

B	**Y**	**I**	**T**
I	O	M	E
R	U	M	M
T	T	E	P
H	H	R	T
		S	A
		I	T
		O	I
		N	O
			N

As we study through the "Life of Christ", our primary text will be the book of Luke. Important events in other gospels not mentioned by Luke will be inserted where they fit chronologically. Why Luke? Well . . . l) Luke is most like the other gospels (only 7% unique material). 2) Luke is chronological, where Matthew and John are not totally. And 3) Luke also wrote the book of Acts, which we'll be studying next.

BIRTH

THE SERIES OF VISIONS

l) The vision of Zachariah (Luke 1:5-25).

Zachariah was an aged priest of blameless life. While engaged in his duties in the temple, the angel Gabriel appeared to him and announced that their prayers would be answered in the birth of a son to his wife Elizabeth. As a sign and seal of the promise, he was to be dumb until its fulfillment.

2) The vision of Mary (Luke 1:26-38).

Elizabeth had a cousin, Mary, of the lineage of David. She was unmarried, though betrothed to a man named Joseph. To her the same angel was sent with the glad message that she, too, should bear a son. He would be called the Son of God, and be the Saviour of men. The Lord God would give Him the throne of His father David, and He would reign over the house of Jacob forever (see 2 Samuel 7:16). He was to be given the name "Jesus", which means "Savior".

Overwhelmed with joy, she journeyed about one hundred miles from Nazareth to the hill country of Judah to be with her cousin, Elizabeth (Luke 1:39-56). What a joyous time these two had, as they pondered what the Lord was about to accomplish through them.

Not long after this John was born (Luke 1:57-66), and although the friends and relatives wished to name him after his father, Zechariah and Elizabeth insisted that his name be "John". At this Zechariah's voice came back to him so that he could speak again. His first words were of praise to God for what He was about to do (see Luke 1:67-79).

3) The vision of Joseph (Matthew 1:18-23).

Among the Jews betrothal was as sacred as marriage, and Mary's apparent violation exposed her to much disgrace. But Joseph was a righteous man and did not want to expose her to public disgrace. He planned to divorce her quietly but after he had considered this, God communicated to him in a dream, and, as a result, he took Mary at once to be his wife. The baby was to be called "Immanuel" — which means, "God with us" (Isaiah 7:14).

BIRTH AND INFANCY

God brings to pass what the prophets had spoken. Micah said that Bethlehem was to be the birthplace of Jesus (Micah 5:2-5), for He was of the family of David. But Mary lived in Nazareth, a town one hundred miles away. God saw to it that Imperial Rome sent forth a *decree* to compel Mary and Joseph to go to Bethlehem, just as the Child was to be born (Luke 2:13). Isn't it wonderful how God uses the decree of a pagan monarch, Caesar Augustus, as an instrument to bring to pass His prophecies! God still moves the hand of rulers to do His will.

When Joseph and Mary arrived in *Bethlehem*, the only available place for them was a stable, probably under the inn. It was here that Jesus was born and laid in a manger (Luke 2:4-7). Such an important event, and yet unnoticed by mankind.

Earth was unconscious of the advent of her King; but heaven could not keep silent. *Angels* brought the glad tidings, and sang their song of "peace on earth"; not to kings and courts, not to proud priests, or pompous Pharisees, but to lowly shepherds who made their way to his lowly cradle (Luke 2:8-20), and were the first on earth to do homage to the World's Redeemer. They were the forerunners and representatives of the common people who "heard him gladly," and who constituted the bulk of his disciples.

The *circumcision* and *naming* occurred, according to Jewish law, on the eighth day (Luke 2:21). At the end of forty days they went to Jerusalem to *present Jesus to the Lord* (see Exodus 13:1,2,11-15), and to perform the *rite of purification* for Mary (Luke 2:21-40; see Leviticus 12:1-8). It was during this visit to the temple that the aged Simeon and Anna recognized Jesus as the Christ and joyously praised God for what was about to happen in Israel.

After Jesus' birth, *Magi* from the east came to Jerusalem asking where the newly born "King of the Jews" was (Matthew 2:1-12). They wished to worship Him. This disturbed King Herod very much. Upon discovering that Bethlehem was the place, Herod told the Magi to find the child and report back to him so that he could worship Him also (however, he intended to kill Him). After worshiping the child (who was probably around one year old), and presenting gifts to Him, the Magi returned to their country by another route.

After the Magi departed, the Lord appeared to Joseph in a dream (Matthew 2:13-18) and told him to take his family to *Egypt,* which he did (see Hosea 11:1). Not long after this, Herod realized that the Magi were not going to report back to him, so he issued a decree to kill all the boys in Bethlehem and its vicinity who were two years old and under (see Jeremiah 31:15).

After Herod's death, an angel told Joseph to take his family back to the land of Israel (Matthew 2:19-23). Fearing Herod's son Archelaus, who reigned in Judea, Joseph took the family to *Nazareth*, in Galilee (see map on page 10).

YOUTH

We have only one scriptural reference to Jesus from the beginning of His stay in Nazareth (age 2 to 3) to the beginning of His ministry (age, approximately 30). Luke 2:41-52 tells of the family trip to Jerusalem for the Passover Feast. In heading back home after the Feast, Joseph and Mary realized that Jesus was not with them. After three days they found Him *in the temple discussing with the teachers.* They were upset with Him, but He simply said, "Didn't you know I had to be in My Father's House?"

This reveals that He must have known, partly at least, the purpose of His mission. Nevertheless, He returned to Nazareth and resumed His simple life. For the next eighteen years He worked as a *carpenter* in Nazareth (Mark 6:3).

IMMERSION

Four centuries had passed since the last voice of public prophecy. The last Hebrew prophet, Malachi (3:1; 4:5,6) as well as Isaiah (40:3), had foretold a *forerunner* of the Messiah. At the annunciation, and again at his birth, *John* had been pointed out as that forerunner. After the detailed account of his birth and circumcision, a single verse (Luke 1:80) contains all that is recorded of him for thirty years. He was to be a Nazarite from birth (Luke 1:15; cf. Num. 6:1-5); and when he emerged from the desert it was in clothing like the prophets of old; made of camel's hair,. with a leather belt around his waist.

John's ministry was preparatory. His theme was, "Repent, for the kingdom of heaven is near" (Matthew 3:2). He said that he was not the Christ, or the prophet, but "the voice of one calling in the desert, 'make straight the way for the Lord' " (John 1:21-23). He came in the "spirit and power of *Elijah*" (Malachi 4:5,6; Luke 1:17) "to make ready a people prepared for the Lord." To emphasize his message he baptized with the b*aptism of repentance for the forgiveness of sins*, at the same time calling men to believe on Him who was to come, and who was to baptize with the Holy Spirit (Luke 3:16; Acts 19:4).

The apex of his ministry came one day when Jesus came to him to be baptized. This strong prophet who would confidently stand up to rebuke the sins of anyone, bowed with deep humility before Jesus. John said, "I need to be baptized by You, and do You come to me?" Jesus replied, "Let it be so now; it is proper for us to do this to fulfill all righteousness" (Matthew 3:13-15).

Jesus had no sins to receive forgiveness from, or to repent of. He simply wanted to "fulfill all righteousness." As Jesus was coming up out of the water, heaven was opened and the Holy Spirit descended on Him in bodily form like a dove. And a voice came from heaven: "you are my Son, whom I love; with You I am well pleased" (Luke 3:21,22; Matthew 3:16,17).

It was at this moment that Jesus became the "Christ". "Christ" simply means "anointed one". Jesus was now anointed by God

Himself in the form of the dove representing the Holy Spirit. He was now ready to go out and accomplish the purpose for which He was sent.

TEMPTATION

Jesus was now on the threshold of His great ministry. He had one more preparatory act before His public ministry would begin. Jesus, now full of the Holy Spirit, was led by the Spirit into the desert, where for forty days He ate nothing and was tempted by the devil (Luke 4:1-13).

First Satan said, "If you are the Son of God, tell this stone to become bread." But Jesus knew that being a Son did not bring demands of the Father but obedience. And His power was not to be used to serve Himself, but others. So, He quoted the book of Deuteronomy (8:3), and said, "Man does not live on bread alone."

Second, Satan showed Jesus all the kingdoms of the world and said, "If you worship me, it will all be yours." But Jesus came to rule in a spiritual way, not a physical one. So . . . He again quoted from Deuteronomy (6:13), "Worship the Lord your God and serve Him only."

Third, Satan took Jesus to the highest point of the temple, and said, "If you are the Son of God, throw yourself down from here." At this point Satan quoted scripture at Jesus, reminding Him of God's care. But Jesus did not have to astonish the crowds to accomplish His purpose. Nor did He need to be presumptuous toward His Father. He simply said, "Do not put the Lord your God to the test," which again was a quote from Deuteronomy (6:16). Scripture then says that Satan left Jesus until an opportune time. Opportune times must have been many in Christ's life for we know that He was "tempted in every way, just as we are — yet without sin" (Hebrews 4:15).

Notice how Jesus defeated Satan! He quoted scripture! He knew the essence of David's saying, "I have hidden your Word in my heart that I might not sin against you" (Psalms 119:11). Honestly, how much scripture do you have committed to memory? How serious are you about defeating Satan?

So . . . Jesus was prepared! He spent thirty years preparing Himself for a three year ministry!

WHAT ABOUT ME?

HAVE I PREPARED MYSELF TO BE AN "ENTREPRENEUR" IN CHRIST'S KINGDOM?

"Entrepreneur" — "A person who organizes and manages a business undertaking, boldly and energetically assuming the risk for the sake of the profit."

As a Christian, God has given us gifts and talents in order to further His kingdom. This is our undertaking — the furtherance of God's Kingdom. We therefore must organize and manage our gifts and talents for kingdom qoals. *boldly* and *energetically* assuming the risk for the sake of the profit.

Look at the parable of the talents — Matthew 25:14-30. What is the point of this parable? The point is this: God has given us gifts/talents that we must invest in His Kingdom. That is our undertaking! Those who are faithful in this undertaking hear, "Well done, good and faithful servant." Does it matter the extent of the gifts/talents which God has given us? No! The point is: Do the best with what you've been entrusted with! And let God do the rest.

So . . . what are your gifts/talents? And how can you better prepare yourself to use them to be God's entrepreneur at work, at home, with friends and relatives, etc., etc.?

POPULARITY DURING CHRIST'S MINISTRY

REVIEW

P	B	Y	I	T
P				
O				
S				
T				

INTRODUCTION

At the end of our last lesson we saw Jesus as the Anointed Son, prepared to embark on the mission for which His Father had sent Him. In this lesson, Jesus begins His ministry with great crowds of people following Him, and wanting to be near Him. Therefore, this period of Christ's life is entitled "Popularity."

Our acrostic for the period of "Popularity" is:

P	A	K		N	A			M	S	
O	U	I	T	I	P	S	O	O	T	T
W	T	N	E	C	O	E	N	U	I	H
E	H	G	A	O	S	R		N	L	E
R	O	D	C	D	T	M	T	T	L	
	R	O	H	E	L	O	H		I	S
	I	M	I	M	E	N	E		N	T
	T		N	U	S				G	O
	Y		G	S						R
			S							M

At the beginning of Christ's ministry we see three reoccurring themes: l) Power, 2) Authority, & 3) Kingdom teachings.

POWER & AUTHORITY

Before anyone would listen to His new teachings, Jesus had to prove that He was from God and that He had the authority to teach these new things. He proved this simply by showing His great power. *His power verified that He had the authority to say what He said.*

Jesus' POWER was manifested in many ways. He was continually *healing* the sick (fever, leprosy, paralytic, shriveled hand, hemorrhage, etc., etc.), which proved His power over sickness. He even *resurrected* the dead (7:11-17; 8:49-55), which proved His power over death. And His power over nature was shown when He calmed the storm (8:22-25), and when He told Simon where to fish, and Simon caught so much that he needed help from another boat to bring it in (5:4-7).

Jesus' AUTHORITY was also shown in many ways. He first claimed authority by reading a passage from *scripture* to those in attendance at the synagogue and claiming that He was the fulfillment of the passage (4:16-21). He next showed His authority by casting out a *demon* (4:31-37). The demon himself even verified the authority of Jesus by saying, "What do you want with us, Jesus of Nazareth? Have You come to destroy us? I know who You are — the Holy One of God!" He even showed authority over *sins* by forgiving the sins of the paralytic (5:17-21), and the sinful woman (7:36-50).

The themes of Power and Authority run side by side all throughout Jesus' period of popularity. One day as He was teaching, a paralytic was brought to Him to be healed (5:17-26). Jesus simply said, "Friend, your sins are forgiven," which brought some opposition from the Pharisees and teachers of the law. So Jesus responded to them, "That you may know that the Son of Man has authority on earth to forgive sins . . .". He said to the paralyzed man, "I tell you, get up, take your mat and go home," which he did. In effect, Jesus was saying "To prove that I have authority to forgive sins, watch this!" His *power* to heal *verified* his *authority* to forgive.

And look at the results:
4:37 — "The news about Him spread"
5:1 — "People crowding around Him"
5:15 — "Crowds of people came to hear Him"
5:26 — "Everyone was amazed and gave praise to God"
7:16 — "A great Prophet has appeared among us"
7:17 — "This news about Jesus spread throughout Judea and the surrounding country"
8:4 — "A large crowd was gathering"
8:40 — "A crowd welcomed Him"
8:42 — "The crowds almost crushed Him"

So . . . Jesus proved that He had power and authority over sickness, nature, demons, sins, and even death. He obviously was the "Son of God." The crowds were truly convinced.

KINGDOM TEACHINGS

Once the King had the attention of the people and had proven that He had power and authority over all things, it came time for Him to teach His subjects what life in His Kingdom would be like. In fact, at one point, Jesus said, "*I must preach the good news of the Kingdom of God to the other towns also, because that is why I was sent*" (4:43). So . . . a common theme throughout all of Christ's teachings (see 8:1; 9:2; etc.) was that *He was preparing people for the coming of His Kingdom*, which was (and is) the church (which means that as Christians today we're a part of His Kingdom and should pay close attention to the "Kingdom teachings").

What does it mean to be a part of Christ's Kingdom? It means that we will be blessed by God if we are *persecuted* for the sake of Christ (6:22, 23). It also means that we should *love* our enemies (6:27), and do to others as we would have them do to us (6:31). We should *forgive*, and not condemn (6:37). We should be *bearing* the *fruit* of good works through our Christian (Kingdom) lifestyle (6:43-45), and we should only call Jesus "*Lord*" if we are doing what He has told us to do (6:46).

The first half of our acrostic for this lesson has to do with the *themes* of Power, Authority, and Kingdom teachings throughout Christ's period of "popularity". The last half of the acrostic is concerned with the *major events* in Christ's life during this time. Although many, many important events took place throughout Christ's life, during each lesson we'll take a close look at the major events which stand out in the period of His life that we'll be studying.

NICODEMUS
John 3:1-21

By all worldly standards Nicodemus was a wise man. He was a Pharisee, which suggested that he was a religious man and that he was also well versed in scripture. He came to Jesus at night to discuss Jesus' actions. Jesus took advantage of the opportunity to do some kingdom teaching. He said, "Unless a man is born again, he cannot see the Kingdom of God." After some questioning from Nicodemus as to how this could happen, Jesus went on to explain that every person in the world has a fleshly birth, which makes them children of their parents. But to be a part of His Kingdom a second (spiritual) birth must occur, which makes us children of God. The emphasis was not on reformation, but on *transformation* — not on improving one's present state, but on completely changing one's status by putting total trust in Christ Himself.

But how could this practically take place? We'll let scripture's golden text speak for itself:

"For God so loved the world that He gave His one and only Son, that whoever believes in Him shall not perish but have eternal life. For God did not send His Son into the world to condemn the world, but to save the world through Him. Whoever believes in Him is not condemned, but whoever does not believe stands condemned already because he has not believed in the name of God's one and only Son" (John 3:16-18).

APOSTLES
Luke 6:12-16

Early in His ministry Jesus personally recruited some special disciples to come and follow Him (Luke 5:1-11, 27-32). After this Jesus had so many disciples that it came time to choose those who would be with Him continually. If Jesus' ministry would continue after His death, it would be through these special men, so He spent the whole night praying to God. When morning came, He called His disciples to Him and chose twelve of them, whom He also designated *apostles*: Simon (whom He named Peter), his brother Andrew, James, John, Philip, Bartholomew, Matthew, Thomas, James son of Alphaeus, Simon who was called the Zealot, Judas son of James, and Judas Iscariot. Jesus was to spend countless hours with these men, preparing them to establish His Kingdom on earth (the church).

SERMON ON THE MOUNT
MATTHEW 5:1-7:29

Remembering that Matthew wrote to Jews to convince them that Jesus was their King helps us to understand the Sermon on the Mount. You see, every kingdom must have its laws and standards to control its subjects. The Kingdom of God is no exception, so, from the lofty pulpit of a mountain, Jesus preached this sermon that contains the laws of His Kingdom.

The three basic themes that stand out in the Sermon on the Mount are: 1) Humility, 2) Love, and 3) Lordship. Don't these three words give us a fit description of Jesus Himself? Yes, yes, a resounding YES! So . . . Jesus taught Kingdom teaching, and lived Kingdom living. And He expected His disciples to do the same!

STILLING THE STORM
Luke 8:22-25

The one event that affected the lives of the apostles more than any other during Jesus' period of popularity was when He calmed the storm. It happened one day as He and the apostles were crossing the Sea of Galilee. Jesus fell asleep, receiving some well-deserved rest. As they sailed, a storm came on the lake, so that the boat was being swamped. The apostles had experienced Jesus' great power, but this was obviously too much. They did not wake Him for help, but to inform Him that they were all about to drown. He rebuked the wind and the raging waters. The storm subsided, and all was calm. All . . . but the minds and hearts of the apostles, who asked each other in fear and amazement, "Who is this? He commands even the winds and the water, and they obey Him." Their faith had been tested, and they all failed. However, it was an experience that they would never forget.

WHAT ABOUT ME?

The King has come! He has given us the laws of His Kingdom! Oh yes, we love Him as our Savior, but do we love Him as our King, and Lord? Take a look back at some of the standards for Kingdom living. How do you rate as a subject of the King? Seriously, what one thing will you earnestly pray about this week — an area in your life where the King needs to reign?

OPPOSITION TO CHRIST'S MINISTRY

REVIEW

P
B Y I T
P
P A K
N A M S
O
S
T

INTRODUCTION

At this point in the life of Christ we have seen the periods of preparation and popularity. Although He remained quite popular among the common people, the Jewish leaders began to become jealous of Jesus and began to oppose Him fiercely. Thus, the third period in Christ's life is called the period of "*OPPOSITION*". This period is the largest of all of the 5 periods (almost 13 chapters — Luke 9:7-21:38). Because of its length we have put together two lessons to cover its material. This lesson will concern itself with the two major themes throughout this period, with our next lesson covering the major events.

Our acrostic for the period of "OPPOSITION" is: "*OBED*".

O	**B**	**E**	**D**
OPPOSITION	BUILDS	EQUIPPING	DISCIPLES

OPPOSITION BUILDING

In the period of popularity we saw a few instances of slight opposition from the Jewish religious leaders. They were trying to figure Jesus out: Who was He, and what was His purpose?, These were their major concerns. Things change however, as they become more and more jealous of His great popularity among the common people. As your teacher leads you through the following passages, notice the progression of opposition to Christ's ministry. Room has been given for your notes.

10:25

11:37-54

13:10-17

14:1-6

15 : 1,2

16 : 14

19:45-48

20:1,2

20:19

20:20-26

20:46,47

So . . . we find at the beginning of this period the leaders were simply "testing" Jesus. But after He rebuked them severely (11:37-54), they began to oppose Him fiercely. Finally, they actually looked for ways to kill Him, or to hand Him over to the power and authority of the governor. In the next period of His life, the period of "suffering", we'll learn that these religious leaders finally were successful in their attempts.

EQUIPPING DISCIPLES

In our last lesson we pointed out the importance of Jesus choosing His apostles. They were to be the ones to actually establish (through His power) His Kingdom, the Church. So . . . as the opposition arose and began to become fierce, Jesus realized that He must work hard to train and equip these men to continue the mission even after He was gone. This is actually just an extension of Christ's "Kingdom Teachings" from last lesson. As your teacher leads you through some of the following passages make any appropriate notes in the space provided.

9:18-27

9:57-62

10:1-17

11:1-13

12:1-12

12:13-40

13:1-9

14:25-35

17:1-10

18:1-8

18:31-33

21:5-19

Wow! This is radical stuff! Jesus was demanding commitment! He wasn't establishing a religion, but a Kingdom under His rule and authority. It meant total commitment to the King, a giving of all to the Lordship of our Master!

WHAT ABOUT ME?

Twice through this section Jesus said that if someone wanted to be His disciple he "must deny himself and take up his cross daily and follow me" (9:23; 14:27). What does it mean to "take up our cross?"

The disciples had probably seen a man "take up his cross", and they knew what it meant. When a man from one of their villages took up a cross and went off with a group of Roman soldiers, he was on a one-way journey. He was walking to his death. Maybe today we should say, "Take up your electric chair" (or gas chamber). The cross was not at this time a symbol of Christ's shed blood. It was simply a symbol of death. So . . . therefore it means the utmost in self-denial. And notice it is to be done daily.

Anyone desiring to become Christ's disciple must daily be willing to put his own interests and wishes into the background and accept voluntarily and wholeheartedly the sacrifice and suffering that will be endured in His service. The "cross" is not the ordinary human troubles and sorrows that all mankind experiences, but the persecution, self-sacrifice, and suffering Christians experience as a result of true faith in and obedience to Him.

So . . . ask yourself, "What about me? — Do I die daily and let Christ truly rule over my life?"

OPPOSITION TO CHRIST'S MINISTRY — PART 2

REVIEW

P

B Y I T

P

P A K

N A M S

O

O B E D

S

T

INTRODUCTION

Our last lesson took us through the two major themes in the period of "Opposition"; "Opposition Building" and "Equipping Disciples". This lesson will cover the major events in this period. There are twelve, so we won't be able to spend much time on each. So . . . strap on your seat belt, cuz we're really going to travel.

Our acrostic for the period of "Opposition", Part 2, is: FeW PeTS LeT RoRy SiTT.

FeW		PeTS			LeT		RoRy		SiTT		
Feeding 5,000	Walking on water	Peter's confession	Transfiguration	Good Samaritan	Lord's prayer	Three parables	Raising Lazarus	Rich young ruler	Shorty	Triumphal entry	Temple Clearing

FEEDING THE 5,000
Luke 9:10–17

Jesus had sent the Apostles out on a mission of healing and preaching. When they returned and reported their successes to Him, Jesus wanted to get away to a secluded place to spend personal time with them. So . . . they took a boat and crossed the Sea of Galilee.

The crowd saw where Jesus was heading, and followed Him by land around the lake. Jesus welcomed them and spoke to them about the Kingdom of God. Finally late in the afternoon the Apostles came to Jesus and told Him to send the crowds away so that they could buy food and find lodging for the night. Jesus tested them by telling them to feed the crowd. They saw no possible way of doing this, so He showed them that He was King of impossibilities by feeding the 5,000 men (no women and children were counted) with 5 loaves of bread and 2 fish.

The people were so filled with excitement that they wanted to take Jesus and immediately make Him King (John 6:14,15). This was one of the temptations Jesus endured in the wilderness. Again He resisted by dismissing the crowd and withdrawing into the hills to pray.

WALKING ON WATER
Matthew 14:22-33

While Jesus dismissed the crowd, He also sent the disciples across the lake by boat. After He had spent some time in prayer, He came to them, walking on the water. At first they were terrified, thinking that He was a ghost. After He reassured them that it was He, Peter called out, "Lord, if it's You, tell me to come to You on the water". To which Jesus replied, "Come". Peter walked on water until he got distracted, then he began to sink. With the Lord's help, he made it back into the boat. Peter learned a great lesson: With his focus on Jesus he could do anything! But when the distractions of life got in his way, he began to sink. Oh, what a great lesson we can learn from Peter's experience.

PETER'S GREAT CONFESSION
Luke 9:18-22

The end of His ministry was now approaching. He had never come right out and claimed to be the Messiah. He had preferred to let the truth dawn gradually on people's minds through His works, His teachings, and His life. But finally the time had come to test the results. So . . . He asked His disciples, "Who do the crowds say I am?" They responded, "John the Baptist" (see Matthew 14:1,2), "Elijah" (see Malachi 4:5,6), and "one of the prophets of long ago" (see Deuteronomy 18:18,19; also the apocryphal book of 2 Esdras predicted the return of Isaiah and Jeremiah — 2:18).

Then He asked, "Who do you say I am?" It was Peter who spoke, not only for himself, but for the twelve, and said, "the Christ of God". In this small group Jesus saw the beginning of His future church. He was very joyous to see that they were beginning to understand who He was and what He was about.

TRANSFIGURATION
Luke 9:28-36

Jesus continued to reveal more of Himself to His disciples. This time He chose three of them, Peter, John and James, and took them up onto a mountain to pray. While there He was transfigured before their very eyes. The Greek word for "transfiguration" is the word that we get the word "metamorphosis" from. So . . . Jesus completely changed before them. Two men also appeared with Him, Moses and Elijah. Here the Old Covenant was coming to meet the New. With Moses representing the Law and Elijah representing the Prophets, they came to meet the One who came to fulfill the entire Old Testament. And what did they talk about? They talked about His one most important act — His redeeming death on the cross. Then a cloud enveloped them, and they heard a voice saying, "This is my Son, whom I have chosen; listen to Him".

There is no doubt but that this experience strengthened Jesus for what was ahead. The voice was for Him a sort of seal of approval. But the event also met a need for the disciples. They were told quite convincingly that Jesus was God's Son and that they were to listen to Him. This experience strengthened the disciples during the days before and after the crucifixion (see I Peter 1:16-18).

THE GOOD SAMARITAN
Luke 10:25-37

To show an expert in the law that everyone was his neighbor, Jesus told a story about a man who was robbed and beaten and left to die. When a priest, and then later a Levite (both religious leaders), saw the man they simply passed by. But a Samaritan (Jewish half-breed) saw him, took pity on him, bandaged his wounds, took him to an inn and took care of him. Then Jesus asked the expert in the law, "Which of these three do you think was the real neighbor?" The man replied, "The one who had mercy on him". Jesus simply said, "Go and do likewise."

What a statement this parable makes on the issue of involvement in other peoples' lives. The priest and Levite selfishly thought of the hassles that would come if they stopped to help this man. Things such as ceremonial defilement if they touched the man and he was dead; time and money both spent helping the man; etc., etc. But instead of thinking selfishly, the heart of the Samaritan went out to the man in such a way that clouded all possible hassles. He saw a need and did everything in his power to meet it. Oh, that we would have such a heart for others!!!

THE LORD'S PRAYER
Luke 11 :1-13

Seeing Jesus continually in prayer, the disciples asked Jesus to teach them how to pray. Four major aspects of prayer are stressed:

l) God's Greatness — "Father, hallowed be Your Name,
2) His Purposes Fulfilled — Your Kingdom come.
3) Our Physical Needs — Give us this day our daily bread.
4) Our Spiritual Needs — Forgive us our sins, for we also forgive everyone who sins against us. And lead us not into temptatation."

Jesus then goes on in the next nine verses emphasizing "persistence" in prayer. He also said, "Ask and it will be given to you; seek and you will find; knock and the door will be opened to you."

THREE PARABLES
Luke 15:1-32

Earlier in His ministry Christ had said, "It is not the healthy who need a doctor, but the sick. I have not come to call the righteous, but sinners to repentance" (Luke 5:31). Now to make this point clear to the Pharisees and the teachers of the law who were muttering about the fact that Jesus would eat with "sinners", Jesus told three parables. The first was about a shepherd who lost one sheep and would leave all the others to go find it. When it was found, he would call his friends together and have a joyous party to celebrate. The next parable was about a woman who lost a special coin. She would sweep the house and search carefully until she found it, then she would celebrate. Each of these parables was followed by the statement that "there is rejoicing in heaven over one sinner who repents."

The third parable (the lost, or prodigal, son) was about a young man who demanded that his father give him his share of the inheritance. When he received it, he set off for a distant country and there squandered his wealth in wild living. After he had spent all of the money, he got a job feeding pigs (can you imagine — a Jew of his day, feeding swine?). Finally, he came to his senses, went back home and begged that his father allow him to be his slave. But his father had other plans. He threw a big party saying "he was dead and is alive again; he was lost and is found". In the same way God is looking for His lost children to come back to Him, and He rejoices greatly when it happens.

RAISING LAZARUS
John 11:1-44

While ministering on the east side of the Jordan River, Jesus received word that His friend, Lazarus, was dying. After two days He set out to go to Bethany, where Lazarus lived. In the meantime, Lazarus had died. When Jesus reached Bethany, He could see the many Jews mourning the death. Martha (Lazarus' sister) told Jesus that if He had only been there, Lazarus wouldn't have died. Jesus replied, "I am the resurrection and the life. He who believes in Me will live, even though He dies". After seeing Mary (Lazarus' other sister) weeping, Jesus' heart went out to His friends. After Himself weeping, He went to the tomb, ordered the stone moved, prayed, and called out, "Lazarus, come out!" Lazarus came out, still wrapped with the burial cloths.

The raising of Lazarus had kindled anew the blaze of popularity on one hand, and the fires of hate on the other. Bethany was only 2 miles from Jerusalem, so this act set the stage for His triumphal entry into Jerusalem, which would take place in only a few days.

THE RICH YOUNG RULER
Luke 18: 18-30

The Jews of Jesus' day associated wealth with God's favor. This makes a rich man's discussion with Jesus even more interesting. After a discussion on what it takes to inherit eternal life, Jesus told the man that he still lacked one thing. He needed to sell everything he owned and give it to the poor. Jesus encouraged him to put his trust in God and not in his own achievements and wealth. The test proved too severe. Christ demanded complete self-surrender to the cause of the Kingdom. The man became very sad, and simply walked away, because he was not willing to give up his great wealth. Oh, "What good is it for a man to gain the whole world, and yet lose or forfeit his very self?" (Luke 9:25).

SHORTY (ZACCHAEUS)
Luke 19: 1-10

In Jericho the chief tax collector was a Jew by the name of Zacchaeus. He had heard of Jesus and wished to see Him. As Christ was passing through Jericho, Zacchaeus, a man of small stature, climbed up into a sycamore tree to get a better view. When Jesus came to the tree, He said, "Zacchaeus, come down immediately. I must stay at your house today."

The method of collecting taxes was open to wide abuse, which made the people regard those in the profession with hatred and contempt. But Jesus didn't care. Zacchaeus had a need and Jesus went to meet it. And when Jesus saw genuine repentance, He said "today salvation has come to this house, for the Son of Man came to seek and to save what was lost."

TRIUMPHAL ENTRY
Luke 19:28-44

Throughout Christ's ministry He had told people and demons alike not to tell that He was the Son of God (4:41; 9:21). He had done this because it was not yet time for His death. But now as He entered Jerusalem it was time to manifest Himself to the people as the King, the Christ, the Messiah. Jesus rode a donkey colt to symbolize that He was a servant of peace, not a warrior king (who would have ridden a horse). Jesus planned the demonstration, even though He knew it would bring on His death. The people shouted for joy as they lay their cloaks and palm branches before Him as He rode. Some Pharisees protested this outburst of enthusiasm. Jesus, in effect, replied that His reign was the event for which the whole history of Israel had been but preparation. The entry has been called triumphant; but He knew well that "Hosannas" would change to "crucify", and palms would be turned into spears. We'll see this actually take place in our next lesson on the period of "suffering."

TEMPLE CLEARING
Luke 19:45-46

From the book of Mark we learn that this incident took place on the day following the triumphal entry. He found people selling and trading in the temple (probably in the court of the Gentiles). So . . . He began to drive them out saying, "My house will be a house of prayer" (Isaiah 56:7), "but you have made it into a den of robbers" (Jeremiah 7:11). .

SUFFERING DURING CHRIST'S MINISTRY

REVIEW

P

P	**B**	**Y**		**I**		**T**
P		**P**	**A**		**K**	
	N	**A**		**M**	**S**	
O						
	O	**B**		**E**	**D**	
	F	**eW**		**P**	**eTS**	
	L	**eT**		**R**	**oRy**	
		S	**iT**		**T**	
S						
T						

INTRODUCTION

Throughout the period of "Opposition" we saw Christ heading for Jerusalem for His eventual death. We also saw the opposition build to a point where the Jewish religious leaders were looking for a way to kill Jesus. In this lesson we'll learn how these men became successful in reaching their goal as we study the period of "Suffering".

This lesson needs the help of all four gospels to give us the "big picture" of Christ's sufferings. We'll still use Luke as our main outline, but much of the material will be coming from other gospels.

Our acrostic for the period of "Suffering" is: "SPATT".

S — last Supper

P — Prayer at Gethsemane

A — Arrested

T — Trials

T — The cross

THE LAST SUPPER
Luke 22: 1-38

When the Day of Unleavened Bread came, the day on which the Passover lamb had to be sacrificed, Jesus sent Peter and John to make preparations for the Passover meal. When it came time for the meal, Jesus had some important things to share with His apostles. Probably most important was that He instituted what we now call the "Lord's Supper". He took some bread and said, "This is My body given for you; do this in remembrance of me". In the same way, He took the cup, saying, "This cup is the New Covenant in my blood, which is poured out for you". There was much symbolism in what Jesus was saying: they had just eaten the Passover meal, which was a remembrance of how the Lord redeemed the Israelites from Egypt by the use of the blood of the lamb (see Exodus 12). But now, the true "Lamb of God" (John 1:29) was about to shed His blood to redeem us from our sins.

After this Jesus told His disciples that one of them was going to betray Him. What a bombshell this must have been to them, except of course Judas, who had already made plans to hand Jesus over to the chief priests (22:3-6).

Jesus let these men see that He loved so much knowing that they would in effect deny Him. At hearing this Peter said, "Lord, I am ready to go with You to prison and to death". Jesus simply replied, "I tell you, Peter, before the rooster crows today, you will deny three times that you know me".

Jesus also told them to get some swords, because it was written, "And He was numbered with the transgressors" (see Isaiah 53:12). He then said, "What is written about Me is reaching its fulfillment".

PRAYER AT GETHSEMANE
Luke 22 :39-46

If Jesus ever needed the support and encouragement of His apostles, this was the time. He knew what was coming; that soon He would be arrested, tried, tortured, and killed. So . . . He leaves the city of Jerusalem and goes out to the Mount of Olives to a garden called Gethsemane. Here He can have the privacy that He desperately needed. After asking the men to pray, Jesus went on a bit further to pray. It was at this point where Jesus had to decide finally that He was going to do things the Father's way. As a man He wanted nothing to do with the cross, so He prayed, "Father, if You are willing, take this cup from me; yet not My will, but yours be done". He prayed with such anguish that His sweat became like drops of blood (this is a rare medical condition called HAEMATIDROSIS). Finally, the decision was made, and He was ready to go on. When He came back to the twelve, they were sleeping, so He told them, "Get up and pray so that you will not fall into temptation".

JESUS IS ARRESTED
Luke 22:47-53

While He was still speaking a crowd (several hundred) came up, and Judas was leading them. He approached Jesus to kiss Him, but Jesus asked him, "Judas, are you betraying the Son of Man with a kiss?", at which Judas simply went through with the betrayal. At this time Peter pulled out a sword and started swinging. He cut off an ear of a servant of the High Priest. But Jesus said, "No more of this", and healed the man's ear. Then Jesus rebuked the religious leaders by asking them why they had not arrested Him while He taught in the temple. He said, "But this is your hour — when darkness reigns," a definite reference to their cold, calloused, evil thinking. After this they arrested Jesus, bound Him, and led Him away. At this the disciples deserted Him and fled (Matthew 26:56)

THE TRIALS
Luke 22:54-22:25

Jesus actually endured six separate trials, three by the Jews, and three by the Roman authorities.

JEWISH TRIALS

The Jews had a definite problem! They wanted to kill Jesus, but did not have the authority of the Roman government to do so. So, they would first do anything to find Him guilty under their law, then they would worry about convincing the Romans to kill Him.

#l) When Jesus was arrested He was taken first to Annas (John 18:13). According to the Jewish law a High Priest would serve until his death. But the Romans had changed this by only allowing a High Priest to serve for only a few years. Caiaphas (Annas' son-in-law) was actually High Priest at this time, but the Jews still left much power and allegience to Annas, so Jesus was brought before him first. Annas questioned Jesus and Jesus calmly and confidently answered him. All through His trials, when Jesus spoke He did so with no fear, remaining calm and confident. It must have seemed to those watching that Jesus was the one actually in control. He had made up His mind in the garden only a few hours before, and now it was time to see it through. At one point Jesus was struck on the face by an official, but still He remained calm.

#2) While Jesus was being questioned by Annas, Caiaphas brought together the Sanhedrin (Jewish supreme court — Matthew 26:57-68). They brought false witness after false witness before the court but could not find two who agreed. Finally two agreed on something that Jesus had said, but it certainly wasn't enough to kill Him for. So, in utter desperation Caiaphas finally said, "I charge you under oath by the living God: tell us if You are the Christ, the Son of God". Jesus replied, "Yes, it is as you say". Now they had a reason to put Him to death. To claim to be God was blasphemy to the Jews. The High Priest tore his clothes, showing total disgust with Jesus. Then they spit in His face and struck Him with their fists. Others played a cruel version of "blind man's bluff" by blindfolding Him and saying "Prophesy! Who hit you?"

The hands they had bound had healed the sick, and raised the dead; the lips they smote had calmed the winds and the waves. One word, and the splendors of the Mount of Transfiguration would have filled the chamber; one word, and the soldiers now sporting with Him at their will would have perished. But, as He had begun and continued, He would end — as self-restrained in the use of His awesome powers on His own behalf as if He had been the most helpless of men. Divine patience and infinite love knew no wearying. He had but to will it and walk free; but He came to die for man, and He would do it.

It was during this time that Peter was asked on three separate occasions, "Weren't you with Him?" You see, Peter had followed along and by the time he denied Jesus the third time he could see the guards beating Jesus. Each time Peter was questioned he became more adamant that he didn't know Jesus, and even called down curses on himself. At this the rooster crowed. The Lord turned and looked straight at Peter. Then Peter remembered the word the Lord had spoken to him: "Before the rooster crows today, you will disown me three times". And he went outside and wept bitterly.

#3) Finally, daybreak broke through. That's right! All the events that we've studied to this point in this lesson happened all night long. At daybreak the Sanhedrin met again to confirm in a legal way the illegal action that had taken place throughout the night. You see, it was illegal for the Sanhedrin to meet at night. Since they wanted to take Jesus to the Roman authorities as soon as possible, especially before the crowds of common people found out what had happened, they quickly met at daybreak and made their official decision. Then the whole assembly rose and led Him off to Pilate.

Before we look at the Roman trials, let's look back at the hypocrisy and illegality of the Jewish trials. 1) It was against Jewish law to punish the accused before he had been proven guilty, but Annas' official struck Jesus. 2) The place was illegal; they should have met in their council chamber. 3) The time was illegal; capital cases could not begin or conclude at night. 4) They probably did not have the required number — a quorum. 5) Once a person was found guilty, twenty-four hours must pass before sentencing him, but not with Jesus. 6) And what about all of the false witnesses? In effect these religious leaders were making a tragic mockery of their own law. The only law that seemed to reign was the law that was written on their selfish, blind hearts that said that Jesus must die, at any cost.

ROMAN TRIALS

#1) Before Pilate. Pilate, as Roman Governor, would be the one that the Jews would have to convince if they were to be successful in killing Jesus. The problem was, however, that Pilate hated the Jews. He would not want to give them their wishes normally, unless his reputation was at stake. He asked Jesus many questions, but found no fault in Him. Finally he heard that Jesus was a Galilean. So, he decided to send Jesus to Herod, the Galilean Governor, who was in Jerusalem at the time.

#2) Before Herod. Herod had one thought in mind; for Jesus to entertain him with some miracles. He gave Him many questions, but Jesus gave him no answer (see Isaiah 53:7). So, he and his soldiers ridiculed and mocked Him, and then sent Him back to Pilate.

#3) Before Pilate again. Now Pilate must decide! The chief priests and teachers of the law were getting louder and more vehement in their attempts to condemn Jesus. Now they were stirring up the crowd to do the same. After some thought Pilate decided to partially give in and have Jesus beaten and then released. But before he could have it done, he had another thought.

Pilate knew Jesus was innocent, so he came up with a new plan. At the Passover each year he would let a prisoner (the peoples' choice) go free. Knowing that many in the large crowd that had gathered would be on Jesus' side, he asks the crowd, "Who should I release, Barabbas (a known robber and murderer), or Jesus?" They yelled for BARABBAS. "What shall I do, then, with Jesus?" Pilate asked. They all answered, "Crucify Him!"

Another problem arose for Pilate: his wife sent him this message: "Don't have anything to do with that innocent man, for I have suffered a great deal today in a dream because of Him" (Matthew 27:19). What questions this must have brought to Pilate's mind.

Then Pilate had Jesus scourged. He was seized by some of the soldiers standing near, and, after being stripped to the waist, was bound in a stooping posture, His hands behind His back. He was then beaten with plaited leather thongs, armed at the ends with acorn-shaped drops of lead, or small, sharp-pointed bones (see Isaiah 1:6 & 53:5). The soldiers then twisted together a crown of thorns and put it on His head (Matthew 19:2,3). They clothed Him in a purple robe and went up to Him again and again saying, "Hail, O King of the Jews!" and kept hitting Him, driving the thorns deeper and deeper into His flesh.

Again Pilate tried to set Jesus free. In his thinking Jesus surely must have suffered enough for whatever He had done. But the Jews kept shouting insults and accusations and "crucify Him" at Jesus. When Pilate saw that he was getting nowhere, but that instead an uproar was starting, he took water and washed his hands in front of the crowd. "I am innocent of this man's blood," he said. All the people answered, "Let His blood be on us and on our children!" So instead of doing what was right the politician Pilate handed Jesus over to be crucified, to please the unruly mob.

THE CROSS
Luke 23:26-56

It was a Roman custom to make the condemned carry his own cross. But Jesus was in no shape to do so. It didn't take long until they had to make another man, Simon of Cyrene, carry Jesus' cross. Upon arriving at the place, Golgotha, the skull, the soldiers got right to the business at hand. The cross was laid on the ground, with Jesus laid (naked) on it. His hands were first nailed to the cross, then His feet. Next the soldiers would lift the top of the cross by ropes until it fell down into the hole that had been prepared for it. Can you imagine the pain as the cross jolted into place? Generally it took days for man to die on a cross — days of excruciating pain! And usually they did not die of a lack of blood. Usually they would die of suffocation. You see, when a person hangs on a cross he can't breath properly without pushing himself up (by pushing on the nail with his feet). After hours of this a person would simply become too exhausted to push up anymore, leading to a suffocating death. Read Psalm 22:1-18 for a detailed prophetical account of the crucifixion.

Christ's mission has almost been accomplished! Just a few more things and he'll be back in His Father's arms. So . . . first He forgives those who were torturing Him. Next, He tells a repentant robber on a nearby cross that he would be with Him today in paradise. Then He asked His close friend John to care for His mother. After darkness had fallen over the whole land, Jesus cried out, "My God, My God, why have you forsaken me?" It was at this point that all the sins of mankind were laid on Jesus' back, and the Father had to turn His back on His only beloved Son. Finally, after receiving a drink, Jesus mustered all of His strength and cried out with a loud voice, "It is finished!" He bowed His head and said, "Father, into Thy hands I commit My Spirit". After saying these things, He yielded up His spirit.

While Christ was on the cross doing these things, the people around the cross were also actively involved. First, a sign was put over Jesus which said, "This is Jesus of Nazareth, the King of the Jews." Then the soldiers gambled for His clothing (see Psalm 22:18). And continually there was the abuse of the passersby, the religious leaders, and the soldiers being hurled at Him.

The gospel of Matthew tells us that at the moment Christ died the curtain of the temple was torn in two from top to bottom. The earth shook and the rocks split. The tombs broke open and the bodies of many holy people who had died were raised to life. These acts led the centurion guarding Jesus to say, "Surely He was the Son of God!"

Jesus' body was taken by a rich man, Joseph of Arimathea, who had been a disciple of Jesus. He wrapped it and placed it in his own new tomb that he had cut out of the rock. Then Pilate stationed soldiers at the tomb so that no one could steal the body and claim that Jesus had been raised from the dead.

SUFFERING DURING CHRIST'S MINISTRY

REVIEW

P

B Y I T

P

P A K

N A M S

O

O B E D

F eW P eT S

L eT R oRy

S iT T

S

S P A T T

T

INTRODUCTION

Christ came to die, and our last lesson showed us how He fulfilled this mission. However, His death would have been meaningless without the Resurrection (see 1 Corinthians 15:12-20). So . . . let's take a good look at Christ's "Triumph" over the grave. Like last lesson, this one will also take advantage of all four gospels, and try to give a complete picture of the recorded events in Christ's period of "Triumph".

Our acrostic for the period of "Triumph" is: RAGG.

Resurrection

Appearances

Great **C**ommission

Going **H**ome

THE RESURRECTION
Luke 24:1-12

The resurrection of the Messiah had been predicted by the prophets (Psalm 16:10; Acts 2:24-31), and even by Jesus Himself (Matthew 16:21; 17:22,23; 20:18,19; Mark 9:9,10; Luke 9:22; John 2:18-22). But the minds of the disciples were so preoccupied with thoughts of a physical kingdom that they could not even come to think of the Christ actually dying. His death, therefore, left them in a very confused and frustrated state. As far as they could figure, all of their hopes were dashed to pieces as Christ died on the cross. If Jesus hadn't risen their hopes would never have been revived, the church would never have been established, and Christianity would never have existed. But He did prove His power over death by leaving His grave empty — let's take a look!

Very early on Sunday morning some women were bringing embalming spices to Jesus' tomb. On their way they were discussing how they could ever roll aside the huge stone from the entrance. But when they arrived they looked up and saw that the stone was already moved away and the tomb was open. Mary Magdalene ran away. But the others entered the tomb and discovered that Jesus' body was gone. While they were wondering about this, suddenly two angels in clothes that gleamed like lightning stood beside them. They said, "Why do you look for the living among the dead? He is not here; He has risen!" So they left the tomb to go and tell the apostles what they had seen and heard (Mark 16:1-4; Luke 24:1-8).

Meanwhile Mary Magdalene had found Peter and John and brought them to the tomb. As they entered the tomb and noticed the strips of linen and burial cloth, they began to believe the resurrection story (John 20:1-9).

POST-RESURRECTION APPEARANCES
Luke 24:13-49

After the resurrection Jesus appeared to His disciples over a period of forty days and taught them about the Kingdom of God (Acts 1:3). It is quite probable that Jesus met regularly with His disciples during this time; however, only eleven post-resurrection appearances are recorded in scripture. It is important to note that the gospel writers were not concerned to narrate the whole history of the resurrection, but to furnish evidences of it.

1) *MARY MAGDALENE* (John 20:10-18). As Peter and John left the tomb and traveled home Mary stayed at the tomb weeping. Upon seeing Jesus, and thinking that He was the gardener, she said, "Sir, if you have carried Him away, tell me where you have put Him, and I will get Him". Jesus said to her, "Mary". She turned to Him, recognizing His voice, and cried out "Rabboni" (which means teacher). She wanted to stay with Him, but He sent her to the disciples to report on what she had seen.

2) *A GROUP OF WOMEN* (Matthew 28:9,10). As the other women traveled from the tomb to tell the disciples, suddenly Jesus appeared before them. He simply told them to tell the disciples to go to Galilee, and that He would meet them there.

3) *THE TWO DISCIPLES ON THE ROAD TO EMMAUS* (Luke 24:13-33). Two disciples were traveling to Emmaus discussing the tragic events of the past week. As they talked, Jesus Himself joined them and, beginning with Moses and all the prophets, He explained to them what was said in all the scriptures concerning Himself. Finally that evening at the table, Jesus took bread, gave thanks, broke it and began to give it to them. Then they realized that it was Jesus, and He disappeared from their sight. They got up at once and returned to Jerusalem.

4) *PETER* (Luke 24:34). We know nothing about this appearance except that the two who walked and talked with Jesus on the road to Emmaus returned to Jerusalem to learn that Jesus had also appeared to Peter.

5) *TEN APOSTLES AND OTHERS* (Luke 24:33-43; John 20:19-23). This is the last appearance that occurred on the day that Christ rose. The disciples were all together that evening discussing the events of the day behind locked doors. Suddenly Jesus appeared in their midst and said, "Peace be with you". After reassuring them that it was truly Him, Jesus ate a piece of broiled fish and then breathed on them the Holy Spirit.

6) *THE DISCIPLES AND THOMAS* (John 20:24-29). Thomas was not present when Jesus appeared at first to the disciples, and he doubted what everyone was saying. So, a week later, Jesus appeared to them again, with Thomas present. Jesus said to Thomas, "Put your finger here; see my hands. Reach out your hand and put it into My Side". Thomas replied, "My Lord and my God".

7) *SEVEN FISHERMEN* (John 21:1-23). The disciples had returned to their old occupation of fishing. After a worthless night, a stranger on shore told them to cast their nets to the right side of the boat. Upon doing it, their nets were full of fish. John realized that it had to be Jesus. Peter was so excited that he jumped overboard and swam ashore. It was at this time that Jesus asked Peter three times if he loved Him. This was in a way a sign of Jesus' forgiveness of Peter's three denials. Jesus commissioned Peter to "feed My Sheep".

8) *500+ IN GALILEE* (Matthew 28:16-20; 1 Corinthians 15:6). Jesus had told His disciples to go to Galilee. He met them there and gave them the "Great Commission".

THE GREAT COMMISSION
Matthew 28:16-20

Until this time, Jesus gave restrictions to His disciples about what they were to say about Him (Luke 9:21). But now the gospel story was complete; Jesus told them to go and make disciples of all nations, baptizing them in the name of the Father and of the Son and of the Holy Spirit, and teaching them to obey everything I have commanded you."

9) *JAMES* (1 Corinthians 15:7). We have no details of this appearance of Jesus to His half-brother.

10) *THE DISCIPLES* (Luke 24:44-49; Acts l:l-8). On this occasion Jesus taught His disciples about things that were to come. He told them to stay in Jerusalem until they had been clothed with the power of the Holy Spirit. Then they were to preach repentance and forgiveness of sins in Jesus' name to all nations (The Great Commission).

GOING HOME (THE ASCENSION)
Luke 24:50-53

11) *THE DISCIPLES* (Mark 16:19; Luke 24:50-53; Acts 1:9-11). Jesus led His disciples out to the Mount of Olives, blessed them, and was taken up to heaven before their very eyes. As they were looking at the sky to catch the last glimpse of Jesus, two angels appeared and said, "Men of Galilee, why do you stand here looking into the sky? This same Jesus, who has been taken from you into heaven, will come back in the same way you have seen Him go into heaven". So, the disciples returned to Jerusalem and waited for the coming of the promised Holy Spirit.

RESURRECTION: HOAX OR HISTORY?

Non-Christians down through the ages have tried to explain away the fact of the resurrection with many very creative theories. Let's take a look at the three most widely-spread theories.

1) *HE WASN'T DEAD!* You've got to be kidding. Jesus was beaten and tortured all night long, scourged (which itself killed many a man), and crucified (don't forget the spear piercing His side), and yet some people think that He was still alive. Preposterous! The soldiers, Pilate, Joseph, Nicodemus, and the crowd were all convinced of His death. And anyway, how could a man in His condition go without food and water for three days and then get up and move a rock that took many men to move? No way! Jesus was truly dead.

2) *THE DISCIPLES STOLE THE BODY.* No way! These were the men who fled when Jesus was arrested. If they would not risk their lives for the living, would they do it for the dead? What about the report of the guard? They witnessed the resurrection, but were bribed to tell a lie about Jesus' body. And what about the disciples themselves? Most of them died as martyrs. Would they die preaching the resurrection if they had actually stolen the body? No way!

3) *JESUS' POST-RESURRECTION APPEARANCES WERE MERE HALLUCINATIONS.* This is ridiculous. Does the same hallucination appear to over five hundred people at the same time? Does a hallucination eat broiled fish right off of the table, or cook fish on the sea shore? Would people be willing to die for a hallucination? I think not!

How about a few more thoughts?

— If it didn't happen, then why would three thousand people respond to Peter's sermon less than two months later (Acts 2)?

— Would the Jews (Christian Jews) have changed their day of worship from the Sabbath Saturday to the Lord's Day (acknowledgment of resurrection) Sunday unless the resurrection was a fact?

NO! NO! NO! NO! NO! All of the theories to disprove the resurrection conclude with a resounding NO! They would not last for a minute in a court of law.

History speaks:

Confucius' tomb:	Occupied
Buddha's tomb:	Occupied
Mohammed's tomb:	Occupied
Jesus' tomb:	*EMPTY!*

The decision is now yours to make. The evidence is quite clear that Christ is indeed risen from the dead! Now what will you do with these facts, accept and spread them (only logical conclusion is that Jesus is God's Son and therefore I must worship and obey Him), or reject and be judged by them?

REVIEW OF CHRIST'S MINISTRY

Fill in each of the following "Review" activities:

P

B Y I T

P

P A K

N A M S

O

O B E D

F eW P eT S

L eT R oRy

S iT T

S

S P A T T

T

R A G G

	KEY WORD	WRITTEN TO WHOM	UNIQUENESS OF BOOK
MATTHEW			
MARK			
LUKE			
JOHN			

THE STRUCTURE OF THE NEW TESTAMENT

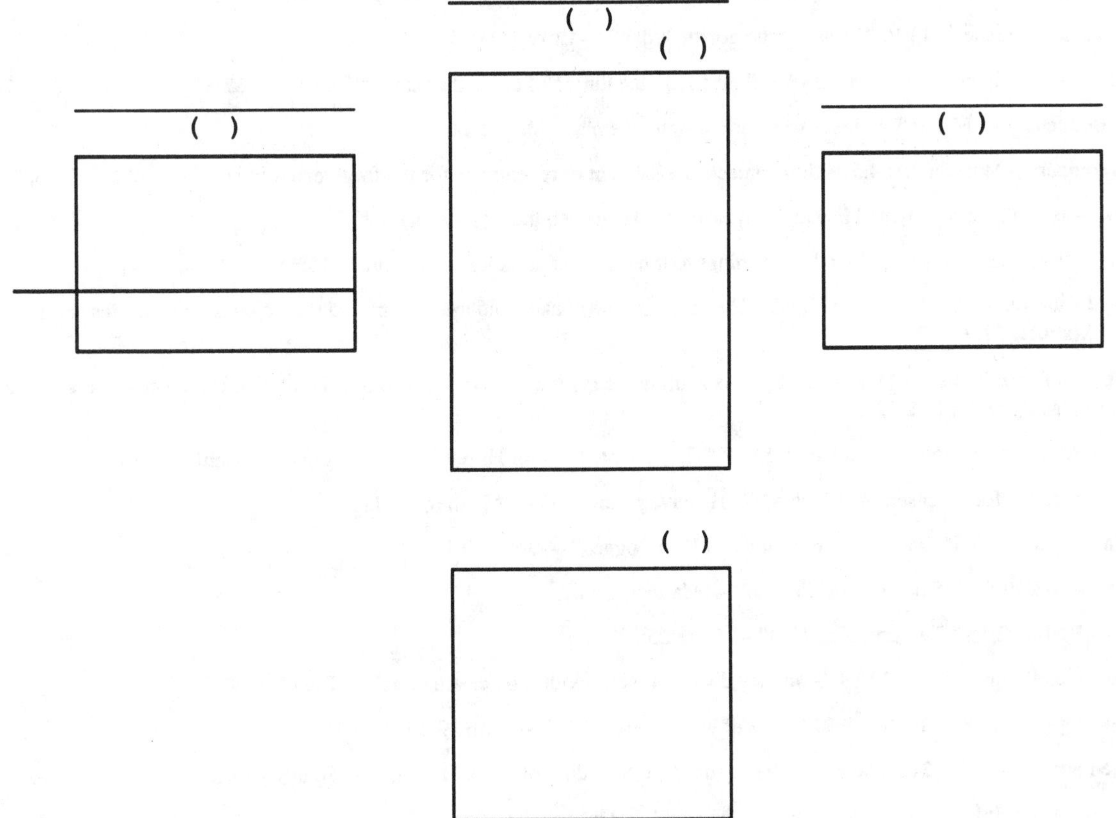

GEOGRAPHICAL MOVEMENTS IN THE "LIFE OF CHRIST"

Turn back to the Life of Christ map on page 10. As your teacher guides you, chart the travels of Christ on this map. *Basically speaking* the travels of Christ go like this: In the period of "Preparation" Jesus went from Bethlehem to Jerusalem, to Nazareth, and then the Jordan River and the desert. For the period of "Popularity" Jesus ministered from Jerusalem, through Samaria, and throughout Galilee. "Opposition" began in Galilee. Then Jesus traveled to Judea, across the Jordan, and finally to Jerusalem. Most of the periods of "Suffering" and "Triumph" took place in or near Jerusalem, except the Great Commission, which took place in Galilee.

PROPHECIES FULFILLED IN JESUS

In the Old Testament (which was completed in approximately 450 B.C.) there are some three hundred distinct prophecies of Jesus Christ that lay like pieces of a jigsaw puzzle. They didn't quite fit until Jesus came and put them together.

What is the probability of all of these prophecies being fulfilled simply by chance, or coincidence? The following probabilities are taken from Peter Stoner in *Science Speaks* (Moody Press, 1963) to show that coincidence is ruled out by the science of probability. Stoner says that by using the modern science of probability in reference to just eight prophecies, "We find that the chance that any man might have lived down to the present time and fulfilled all eight prophecies is 1 in 10^{17}." That would be one in 100,000,000,000,000,000. In order to help us comprehend this staggering probability, Stoner illustrates it by supposing that "we take 10^{17} silver dollars and lay them on the face of Texas. They will cover all of the state two feet deep. Now mark one of these silver dollars and stir the whole mass thoroughly, all over the state. Blindfold a man and tell him that he can travel as far as he wishes, but he must pick up one silver dollar and say that this is the right one. What chance would he have of getting the right one? Just the same chance that the prophets would have had of writing these eight prophecies and having them all come true in any one man, from their day to the present time, providing they wrote them in their own wisdom."

This means that the fulfillment of these eight prophecies alone proves that Jesus is the Messiah. But there are over three hundred prophecies! Let's take a look at a few of them:

1. Born of a Virgin — Isaiah 7:14 "The virgin's name was Mary" — Luke 1:27.

2. Son of Abraham — Genesis 12:3 "Jesus Christ, the Son of David, the Son of Abraham" — Matthew 1:1.

3. Tribe of Judah — Genesis 49:10 "Jesus . . . the Son of Judah" — Luke 3:23,33.

4. Son of David — 2 Samuel 7:16 "The Lord will give Him the throne of His father David" — Luke 1:32,33.

5. Born in Bethlehem — Micah 5:2 "Jesus was born in Bethlehem" — Matthew 2:1.

6. The Forerunner — Malachi 3:1; 4:5,6 "John preached a baptism of repentance for the forgiveness of sins" — Luke 1:17,76,77; 3:3.

7. Miracles — Isaiah 35:5,6 "Laying His hands on each one, He healed them" — Luke 4:40.

8. Parables — Psalm 78:2 "Jesus spoke all these things to the crowd in parables" — Matthew 13:34.

9. Triumphal entry on donkey — Zechariah 9:9 "They brought the donkey and the colt, placed their cloaks on them, Jesus sat on them" — Matthew 21:7.

10. Betrayed by a friend — Psalm 41:9 "One of you is going to betray me . . . the one to whom I will give this piece of bread . . . He gave it to Judas" — John 13:21-26.

11. Sold for thirty pieces of silver — Zechariah 11:12 "They counted out for Him thirty silver coins" — Matthew 26:15.

12. Would not speak before accusers — Isaiah 53:7 "He gave no answer" — Matthew 27:12.

13. Scourging — Isaiah 53:5 "Pilate took Jesus and had Him flogged" — John 19:1.

14. Spat upon — Isaiah 50:6 "They spit in His face" — Matthew 26:67.

15. Pierced — Psalm 22:16 "They crucified Him" — Luke 23:33.

16. Lots cast for clothing — Psalm 22:18 "And they divided up His clothes by casting lots" — Luke 23:34.

17. Offered vinegar to drink — Psalm 69:21 "A jar of wine vinegar . . . " — John 19:29.

18. No broken bones — Psalm 34:20 "He was already dead, so they did not break His legs" — John 19:33.

19. Darkness — Amos 8:9 "Darkness came over all the land" — Matthew 27:45.

20. Buried in rich man's tomb — Isaiah 53:9 "A rich man . . . Joseph . . . placed it in his own new tomb" — Matthew 27:57-60

21. Resurrection — Psalm 30:3 "He has risen" — Luke 24:6.

22. The ascension — Psalm 68:18 "Was taken up into heaven" — Luke 24:51.

JESUS IS THE CHRIST!

JESUS IS GOD!

HE HAS PROVEN IT THROUGH HIS RESURRECTION AND THROUGH FULFILLED PROPHECY! OUR RELIGION IS BASED ON FACT, NOT FEELINGS OR EMOTION! RATIONALLY SPEAKING, "JESUS IS THE WAY AND THE TRUTH AND THE LIFE. NO ONE COMES TO THE FATHER EXCEPT THROUGH HIM" (JOHN 14:6).

WHO DO YOU KNOW THAT NEEDS TO BE CONFRONTED WITH THE *FACTS* OF THE GOSPEL? WHAT WILL YOU DO TO MAKE SURE THAT THEY HEAR THEM? YOU MAY BE THE ONLY BRIDGE TO CHRIST THAT THESE PEOPLE HAVE!!!

THE STRUCTURE OF "ACTS"

". . . YOU WILL BE MY WITNESSES IN JERUSALEM, AND IN ALL JUDEA, AND SAMARIA, AND TO THE ENDS OF THE EARTH."
ACTS 1:8

GEOGRAPHICAL MOVEMENT		CHAPTERS	KEY PERSONALITY	DATES & PASSAGES FOR STUDY	
JERUSALEM		1–7	PETER	4/13	Intro & Ch. 1
				4/20	Ch. 2 & 3
				4/27	Ch. 4-7
JUDEA & SAMARIA		8-12		5/4	Ch. 8-12
THE ENDS OF THE EARTH	PAUL'S MISSIONARY JOURNEYS	13:1–21:14	PAUL	5/11	13:1-15:35
				5/18	15:36-21:14
	PAUL'S IMPRISONMENT	21:15–28:31		5/25	21:15-28:31

INTRODUCTION

In the book of Acts Luke picks up where he left off in his gospel — in giving "an orderly account" (Luke 1:3) of the life of Christ. In Acts 1:1 he writes, "In my former book, Theophilus, I wrote about all that Jesus *began* to do and to teach until the day He was taken up to heaven." Now if his former book, the gospel of Luke, was what Jesus "began" to do, then the books of Acts becomes the continuation of Jesus' ministry. So Jesus is the central figure in both books. In Luke He is the Incarnate Son of God, in the flesh. In Acts He is the Risen Christ, acting powerfully through His Holy Spirit to bring God's salvation to mankind.

"Acts" is a history book, but it is history with a purpose. It is history selectively chosen to show the expansion of God's Kingdom, the Church, from *Jerusalem*, to *Judea* and *Samaria*, and to the *ends of the earth*. Therefore, we don't see a detailed history of each of the apostles, but rather the birth and early growth of Christ's body, the Church.

"Acts" is also the only unfinished book in the Bible. Why? Because as long as Christ lives and works through His Spirit to change lives the story goes on. The "ends of the earth" are still not reached. The book was just the beginning. We today are a continuation of the "Acts".

ACTS — CHAPTER 1

We have already seen that the book of Acts is all about the birth and expansion of the Church. This process actually begins in chapter 2, leaving chapter l as an introduction to the book, or a transition from "Luke" to "Acts".

The first eleven verses are basically review from "Luke", with a few new thoughts added. In "Luke" it appeared that Jesus resurrected and ascended on the same day but Luke tells us here (v. 3) that Jesus appeared to the disciples over a period of forty days. And notice what he spoke about — "The Kingdom of God" — of course (refer to Luke 4:43).

Luke's last words of Jesus give us an outline to the entire book. He said, "You will receive power when the Holy Spirit comes on you; and you will be my witnesses in Jerusalem, and in Judea and Samaria, and to the ends of the earth." Starting with our next lesson, we'll begin to see this process take place. After Jesus' ascension (vs. 9-11) the disciples returned to Jerusalem and patiently waited for the coming of the Spirit, which Jesus had promised (vs. 4-5). They continued in prayer (v. 14) during the ten days between the Ascension and the Day of Pentecost (the day on which the Spirit was sent). During this time Peter took charge of choosing a successor to Judas (vs. 15-26) who had committed suicide (Matthew 27:3-10; Acts 1:18,19). He told the others that the Old Testament had predicted Judas' betrayal, and that they must choose someone to take his place. The person to take this place had to be a companion of the Lord during His whole public ministry, and a witness of His resurrection. They proposed two men: Justus and Matthias. Then they prayed for the Lord's will, and cast lots (which was a method used occasionally to find God's will — Proverbs 16:33). The lot fell to Matthias, so he was added to the eleven apostles.

So now the stage is set! Everything is in place for the coming of the Holy Spirit.

THE BOOK OF ACTS

KEY WORD: CHURCH

Acts represents the birth of the Church (birthday cake). The tongues of fire (large flame on each candle) and other miraculous signs sparked the beginning of the Church. The Church then spreads (arrows) throughout the world (globe), from Jerusalem to Judea, to Samaria, and to the ends of the earth. This process is still not complete, and becomes the responsibility of Christians today.

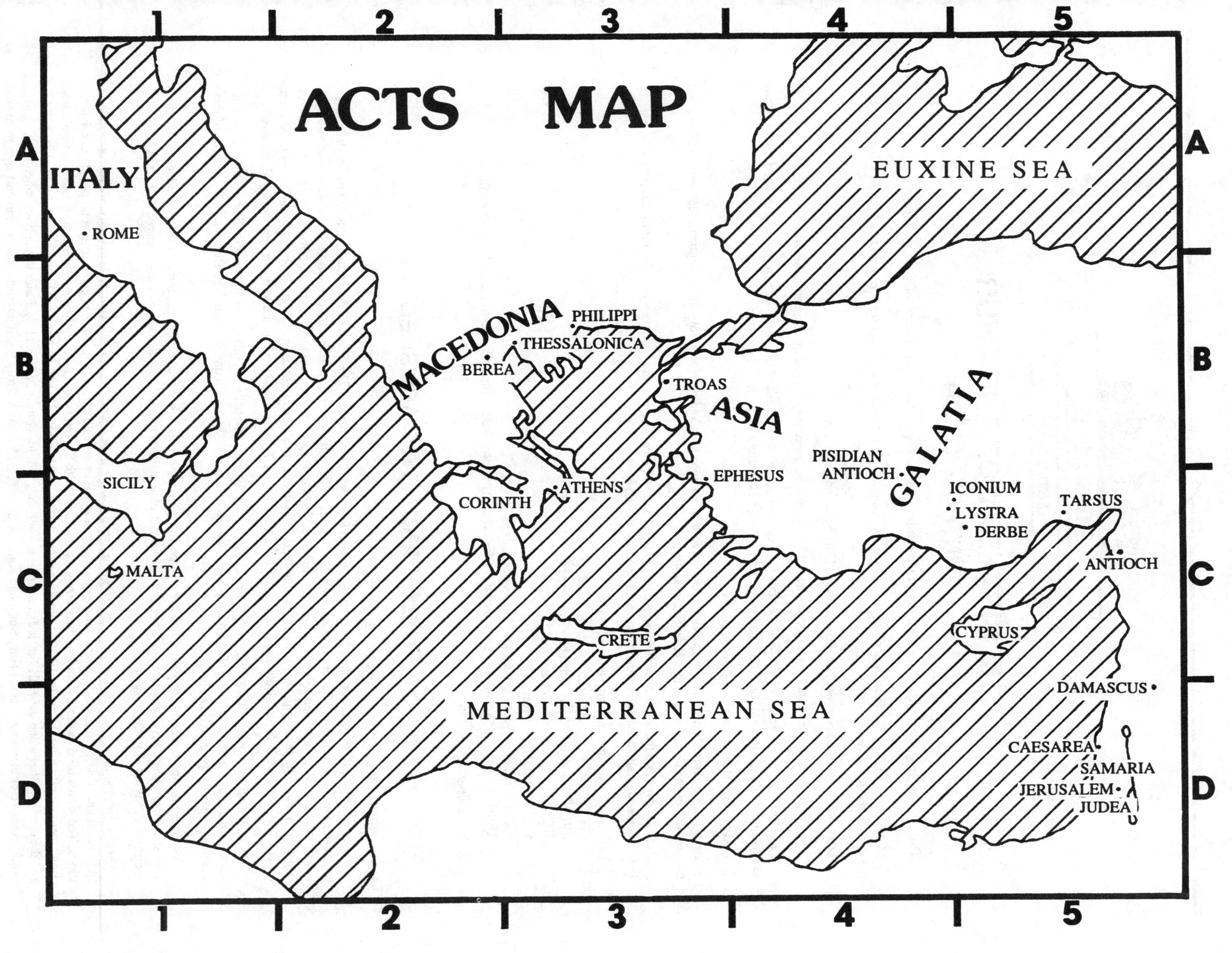
ACTS MAP
ITALY
ROME
SICILY
MALTA
MACEDONIA
PHILIPPI
THESSALONICA
BEREA
CORINTH
ATHENS
TROAS
ASIA
EPHESUS
GALATIA
PISIDIAN ANTIOCH
ICONIUM
LYSTRA
DERBE
TARSUS
ANTIOCH
CRETE
CYPRUS
EUXINE SEA
MEDITERRANEAN SEA
DAMASCUS
CAESAREA
SAMARIA
JERUSALEM
JUDEA

LESSON #12

ACTS 2 & 3

THE BIRTHDAY OF THE CHURCH

INTRODUCTION

Throughout the gospels we can see glimpses of the coming church. Let's take a look at a few of these passages:

Matthew 16:19 says that Peter was given the keys of the Kingdom of Heaven, suggesting that he would be the one to actually open the door to the Kingdom.

Luke 3:16 says that Jesus would baptize with the Holy Spirit and with fire.

Luke 24:47 says that repentance and forgiveness of sins would be preached in Jesus' name, beginning at Jerusalem.

Luke 24:48 says that Jesus would send the apostles what His Father had promised (referring back to Luke 3:16), and that they were to stay in the city (Jerusalem) until they had been clothed with power from on high.

And in our last lesson we saw these passages:

Acts 1:4,5 — Here Jesus told His apostles to stay in Jerusalem until they had received Holy Spirit baptism. He also explained that the promise of the Father was in fact Holy Spirit baptism.

Acts 1:8 says that the apostles would receive power when the Holy Spirit came on them; then they would be Christ's witnesses in Jerusalem, and in all Judea and Samaria. and to the ends of the earth.

Let's see if we can summarize these passages:

CITY:	Jerusalem
EVENTS:	Holy Spirit baptism; Kingdom opened
SIGNS:	Power and fire
KEY PERSON:	Peter
MESSAGE:	Repentance and forgiveness of sins
RESULT:	Apostles to be witnesses of Jesus in Jerusalem, Judea, Samaria. and to the ends of the earth.

Let's see what happens!!!

THE CHURCH IS ESTABLISHED

HOLY SPIRIT BAPTISM — Acts 2:1-13

"When the Day of Pentecost came, the apostles were all together in one place." The Feast of Pentecost came approximately fifty days after Passover (ten days after Jesus' ascension). It was one of the three great annual feasts at which the Jews were required by the law to attend at the temple. Jerusalem was jammed. Indeed, 200,000 people could crowd together in the temple area alone. Estimates range from one to three million people living in or around Jerusalem at this time. (Notice how God plans for great crowds to be present for His "major events". Jesus' death and resurrection took place during Passover, and now the church is begun during Pentecost.)

So, as the apostles were all together on this special day, suddenly some phenomenal things began to occur. The whole house was filled with a sound like the blowing of a violent wind. Tongues of fire rested on each one of them. The Holy Spirit filled each of them, and they began to speak in other languages.

You can imagine the crowd that would gather at such an event, especially when the people realized that these uneducated Galileans were speaking in the native languages of all of those present. Some insisted that the apostles were drunk. Others, more wisely, asked one another, "What does this mean?"

Before we find the answer to that question, let's make sure that we understand *Holy Spirit baptism.* It actually has its roots in the Old Testament. That's right, God's Spirit was frequently mentioned in the Old Testament. He was given to special people in crisis situations. The words used in these instances were terms having to do with the outward manifestations of the Spirit; words such as "came upon" were usually used (1 Samuel 10:10, 11:6; Judges 6:34, 14:6; 1 Chronicles 12:18). In Acts we see these words used also. Jesus had told the disciples that when the Holy Spirit came *on* them, then they would witness of Him (1:8). Later in the book when relating back to this event Peter mentions that the Holy Spirit had come *on* them (11:15). So . . . Holy Spirit baptism was an outward sign from God to the apostles that it was time to preach repentance and forgiveness of sins in Jesus' name. It was His "seal of approval" that the timing was now right. We'll see Holy Spirit baptism one more time in "Acts". It seems that the Jews were reluctant to spread their "good news" to the Gentiles (non-Jews). However, when God sent Holy Spirit baptism upon some Gentiles, they then knew that it met with His approval (chapters 10 & 11). Hebrews 2:3,4 says that God used many signs and wonders (such as Holy Spirit baptism) to show that the salvation that Jesus and the apostles spoke of was really from God Himself.

PETER'S SERMON — Acts 2:14-36

After defending the accusation of drunkenness by pointing out that it was only nine o'clock in the morning, and showing that the prophet Joel had predicted what they now were experiencing, Peter gets to the point — *Jesus is the Christ.*

1) His miracles prove it (22).
2) His death proves it (23).
3) His resurrection proves it (24).
   A. David prophesied it (25-31).
   B. The apostles witnessed it (32).
4) His exaltation to the right hand of God proves it (33).
   A. Holy Spirit baptism proves it (33).
   B. Again David prophesied it (34,35).

CONCLUSION: "Therefore let all Israel be assured of this: God has made this Jesus, whom you crucified, both Lord and Christ" (36).

Not only did Peter call Jesus "Christ", "Messiah", their Savior. He also called Him Lord. When the Old Testament was translated into Greek, the term Lord (*Kurios* in Greek) was used for God's name. Thus in declaring Jesus to be "Lord", Peter clearly identified this crucified and resurrected Messiah with the one true God of Old Testament history. He is Lord!He is God!

WHAT SHALL WE DO? — Acts 2:37-41

The peoples' reaction to Peter's sermon was quite simple — they *believed* Peter's message and therefore felt guilty. So guilty, as a matter of fact, that the Bible says, "they were cut to the heart" (vs. 37). These peoples' hearts were broken as they were made aware of their sin. They wisely asked, "Brothers, what shall we do?"

Peter replied, "Repent and be baptized, every one of you, in the name of Jesus Christ so that your sins may be forgiven and you will receive the gift of the Holy Spirit" (vs. 38). Let's break this verse down to see just what it is saying:

1) *REPENT* — This indicates a "*change*" of direction in a person's life rather than simply a mental change of attitude or a feeling of remorse; it signifies a turning away from a sinful and godless way of life (a very serious decision).

2) *BE BAPTIZED* — Baptism with water had been used by John the Baptist to symbolize repentance and forgiveness of sin. After the resurrection Jesus had commanded His followers to make disciples of all nations and to baptize them in the name of the Father, Son and Holy Spirit (see Matt. 28:19). Now it was time to begin. The word "baptize" has come to mean many things in many churches (ie. sprinkling, pouring, etc.). Originally in the Greek (the New Testament was originally written in Greek) it meant "immerse" or "submerge". An example of this is in Acts 8:36-39 (see also Romans 6:1-11).

3) IN THE NAME OF JESUS CHRIST — Notice that only "in" Christ can the following blessings take place.
   a) *Sins may be forgiven* — it is only through Christ and His sacrifice that our sins can be forgiven.
   b) *Receive the gift of the Holy Spirit* — this does not refer to the miraculous gift which had just been bestowed upon the apostles; for we know from the subsequent history that this gift was not bestowed on all who repented and were baptized, but on only a few brethren of prominence in the several congregations. The expression means the Holy Spirit as a gift; and the reference is to that indwelling of the Holy Spirit by which we bring forth the fruits of the Spirit, and without which we are not of Christ (see Romans 8:9-11; 1 Corinthians 3:16; Galatians 5:22,23). The Spirit would empower them both to live new lives and to continue the ministry and mission of the risen Lord out into the world.

Peter then went on to say, "Save yourselves from this corrupt generation". While it is true that the sinner can do nothing in the way of meriting his own salvation, or of forgiving his own sins, he must do that which is prescribed as the method of accepting the salvation offered to him. To this extent he saves himself.

WOW! Look at the results. Three thousand people accept the message of Peter and become the charter members of the Church.

THE EARLY CHURCH — Acts 2:42-47

The life of this infant church was characterized by four things:

1) *THE TEACHING OF THE APOSTLES.* The apostles had lived with Jesus for three years. During this time He had equipped them to establish His Kingdom on earth. So, they went about fulfilling part of the Great Commission by teaching the disciples all that Jesus had commanded in His "Kingdom Teachings".

2) *FELLOWSHIP.* This is a genuine sharing of common life — their common spiritual blessings through Christ, and their material blessings as well.

3) *BREAKING OF BREAD.* This refers to the remembrance of the Lord in the Lord's Supper.

4) *PRAYERS.* This is nothing new to these Jews, but it took a different twist as now they prayed in Jesus' name (according to His will).

Notice also that there are four results to this kind of church life.

1) *AWE.* Everyone had a deep sense of reverence for what God was doing in their lives.

2) *COMMON SHARING.* If someone had a physical need they would meet it. They realized that all of their possessions were God's and that He wanted them to use the possessions to further the Kingdom.

3) *FAVOR.* Everyone appreciated what they saw from these Christians.

4) *GROWTH.* The Lord added to their number daily those who were being saved.

PETER HEALS THE CRIPPLED BEGGAR — Acts 3:1-10

One day as Peter and John were going to the temple to pray, a lame beggar asked them for money. At this request, Peter said, "Silver or gold I do not have, but what I have I give you. In the name of Jesus Christ of Nazareth, walk." As the crowds of people saw this man walking, and jumping, and praising God, and recognized him as the beggar, they were astonished and gathered around Peter and John.

PETER'S GOSPEL SERMON — #2 — Acts 3:11-26

So again Peter has a crowd to preach to. After explaining that it was not by their own power that the man had been healed, Peter proceeded to preach Christ to them. His first order of business was to convict these people of their sin. They: 1) Handed Jesus over to be killed, 2) Disowned Him (the Holy and Righteous One) before Pilate, 3) Asked that a murderer be released instead, & 4) Killed the Author of Life. Now to prove that Jesus is the Christ, Peter proceeds: 1) They are witnesses of the resurrection, 2) By faith (Peter's faith) in Jesus' name the lame beggar was healed, 3) Fulfilled prophecy: a) Jesus is the "prophet" spoken of by Moses, b) Jesus fulfills the promise to Abraham that through his offspring all peoples on earth would be blessed. How? By turning these people from their wicked ways.

In the middle of this sermon Peter told the people to repent, so that their sins may be wiped out. Although he never actually finished his sermon, we know that Peter got through to many in the crowd that day because the number of male believers grew to about five thousand.

LESSON #13

ACTS 4–7

BOLDNESS FOR JESUS

INTRODUCTION

In our last lesson Peter used the keys given to him by Jesus Himself (Matthew 16:19) to finally open the doors to the Kingdom of Heaven, which is the Church. So now it will become our focus to watch the expansion of the Church "*in Jerusalem, and in all Judea and Samaria, and to the ends of the earth*" (1:8). By taking a quick look at our chart on page 39 we can see that this lesson takes place entirely in Jerusalem. This was a period of time in which the Church grew tremendously, led by the power of the Holy Spirit. It was also a time in which the Word was almost exclusively spread among the Jews. We'll have to look for "Judea, Samaria, and the ends of the earth" in future lessons.

You might remember that at the close of our last lesson we saw Peter healing a lame man and preaching Christ to a large group of people at the temple. Let's see what happens:

PETER'S BOLDNESS

The opposition of the Pharisees is paramount in the Gospels. In the Acts it is the Sadducees who oppose the Christians. This is because the Sadducees disbelieved the doctrine of resurrection which the apostles were preaching so powerfully. In this instance they even used the captain of the temple guard to try to silence Peter's preaching. They seized Peter and John and put them in jail until the next day.

The next day the Sanhedrin met to question Peter and John about the healing of the lame man. So this again gave Peter the opportunity to preach about the risen Savior. In Peter's brief (spirit-filled) answer he pointed out that the miracle was a deed of kindness, not a crime. Then he *boldly* stated that it took place in the name of Jesus Christ of Nazareth. They had crucified Him, but God raised Him from the dead. He pointed out that Jesus' rejection was predicted in the Old Testament. And finally he offered salvation in Jesus' name to those present by saying, "Salvation is found in no one else, for there is no other name under Heaven given to men by which we must be saved" (4:12).

The Sanhedrin had a problem. They did not choose to face the reality of the healing and its implications (the facts of Peter's sermon). Rather they wanted all talk of Jesus to cease, so they commanded them not to speak or teach at all in the name of Jesus, to which Peter and John replied, "Judge for yourselves whether it is right in God's sight to obey you rather than God. For we cannot help speaking about what we have seen and heard" (4:19,20). The Sanhedrin then threatened them, and let them go.

Now where did this sudden burst of *boldness* come from? The Sanhedrin even noticed their great courage! Is this the same Peter that we saw running from Jesus and denying Him in His greatest time of need? NO!!! We now see Peter as a transformed man! Why? Simply because he was "filled with the Holy Spirit." So what is my key for being *bold* and courageous for my Lord? It is simply by living my life under the power and control of the Spirit! Then I'll see great things happen!

THE APOSTLES' BOLDNESS

A SPECIAL PRAYER — Acts 4:23-31

Peter and John left the Sanhedrin and headed straight to be with their Christian brothers. They began to pray, not asking the Lord to remove the threats nor to relieve them of the problem, but to give them boldness to speak His words, and for confirmation of their message by signs and wonders. Immediately their prayer was answered. The place where they were meeting was shaken, and they were all filled with the Holy Spirit and spoke the Word of God *boldly*.

SHARING OF POSSESSIONS — Acts 4:32-37

The people realized that everything that they owned actually belonged to God, so if someone else had a need they would sell what they had to meet the need. Many people sold homes or land and brought the money to the apostles to distribute as needed. A man named Barnabas was one who did this. We'll see more of him in future lessons.

THE SIN OF ANANIAS & SAPPHIRA — Acts 5:1-11

There was one couple that saw a chance for acclaim among the disciples. Their names were Ananias and Sapphira. Their plot was simple: sell some property and give some of the money to the apostles, claiming that it was the full amount. Peter *boldly* rebuked their sin, saying that they had lied to the Holy Spirit. For their sin both Ananias and Sapphira died immediately after hearing Peter's rebuke. The result was that great fear seized the whole church and all who heard about these events. They knew that they were not playing a game. Christianity means serious business!!!

SIGNS AND WONDERS — Acts 5:12-16

Remember that they had prayed for signs and wonders to accompany their message (4:30). In this passage we see that everyone sick in the area around Jerusalem would come to the apostles to be healed. We learn that ALL of them were healed. The result: more and more men and women believed in the Lord and were added to their number.

PERSECUTION FROM THE SADDUCEES — Acts 5:17-42

The Sadducees became so jealous of the apostles that they had them arrested. But in the night an angel of the Lord let them out of prison and told them to continue preaching the full message of this NEW LIFE in the temple courts, which they *boldly* did.

In the morning the Sanhedrin sent for the apostles, but they were no longer in jail. Finally they were found teaching in the temple courts. So, they were brought in to be questioned by the High Priest. He said, "We gave you strict orders not to teach in this name, yet you have filled Jerusalem with your teaching and are determined to make us guilty of this man's blood" (5:28). Their *bold* response was right to the point: 1) We must obey God, 2) God raised Jesus from the dead, 3) You killed Him, 4) God exalted Him to His right hand as Prince and Savior, 5) He offers forgiveness of sins to Israel, 6) We (the apostles) are witnesses of these things, 7) So is the Holy Spirit, and 8) The Holy Spirit is given to those who obey God.

At this the Sanhedrin was furious and wanted to put them to death. But a wise Pharisee named Gamaliel calmed them down by saying, "If their purpose or activity is of human origin, it will fail. But if it is from God, you will not be able to stop these men; you will only find yourselves fighting against God." So they had them flogged (probably 40 times — see Deuteronomy 25:3), ordered them not to speak in the name of Jesus, and let them go.

The apostles left the Sanhedrin, *rejoicing because they had been counted worthy of suffering disgrace for the Name.* How about you? Are you bold enough to put yourself in a position of potential persecution and disgrace for Christ? And when it happens, do you rejoice? The apostles were not affected by the Sanhedrin's threats and punishment. They continued day after day, in the temple courts and from house to house, boldly teaching the good news that Jesus is the Christ.

STEPHEN'S BOLDNESS

As the Church grew so did the possibility of problems rising in their midst grow. One such problem involved the daily distribution of food. You see, there were actually two different groups among the Jews: the Aramaic-speaking Jews living in Judea, and the Grecian Jews who came from other lands and had the attitudes and language of the Greeks. It was these Grecian Jews that complained that their widows were being overlooked in the daily distribution of food. Now this was a serious problem. They could handle the outside persecutions from the Sadducees, which actually served to strengthen their faith. But this inner problem, which could result in division, had to be solved immediately. The apostles insisted that their #1 priority was the ministry of the Word, and prayer. So they suggested that the disciples choose seven men who were full of the Spirit and wisdom, to care for the responsibility of the distribution of the food. These seven were then presented to the apostles, who prayed and laid their hands on them.

One of these men was named Stephen. He was a man full of God's grace and power (it appears that he received this power at the laying on of the apostles' hands). He did great wonders and miraculous signs among the people. However, opposition arose from members of a certain synagogue, who argued with Stephen's teaching, but could not stand up to his wisdom or the Spirit by which he spoke. So, they stirred up the people and the elders and the teachers of the law. They seized him, brought him before the Sanhedrin, produced false witnesses and attempted to discredit Stephen's teachings.

STEPHEN'S SERMON — Acts 7:1-53

When given the opportunity to reply to the charges, Stephen made no attempt to defend himself, but rather defended Christianity as the true fulfillment of the prophetical promises and the Mosaic law. His discourse was actually a review of Jewish history. He began with God's covenant with Abraham. He then filled in a few details up to Moses, and spent much time speaking of Moses and the Mosaic covenant. His next major theme was the tabernacle, which represented God's presence through the times of Joshua, David, and Solomon. Suddenly, Stephen's discourse changed from historical narrative to rebuke. Perhaps he could tell that these men were not really listening to him at all, so he jumped past much history and boldly got right to the point:

"You stiff-necked people, with uncircumcised hearts and ears! You are just like your fathers: You always resist the Holy Spirit! Was there ever a prophet your fathers did not persecute? They even killed those who predicted the coming of the Righteous One. And now you have betrayed and murdered him — you who have received the law that was put into effect through angels but have not obeyed it."

Needless to say the Sanhedrin was not too thrilled to hear these words. They gnashed their teeth at him, covered their ears, yelled at the top of their voices, rushed at him, dragged him out of the city, and stoned him.

While they were stoning him, Stephen prayed, "Lord Jesus, receive my spirit." Then he fell on his knees and cried out, "Lord, do not hold this sin against them." Sounds quite a bit like Jesus' last few words, doesn't it? When he had said this, he fell asleep.

In our next lesson we'll see that a positive result came from the stoning of Stephen. A great persecution arose against the Church which scattered the Christians all throughout Judea and Samaria.

WHAT ABOUT ME?

As your teacher leads you in thinking about your own "boldness" for Christ, jot down some areas of your life where you need to be bolder, and what you will do about it this coming week.

SPREADING THE WORD

INTRODUCTION

Acts 8:1-3

The "Beginning at Jerusalem" (Luke 24:47) has been fulfilled. It is now time to follow the spread of the church throughout the geographical regions of Judea and Samaria. But how would this happen? It is interesting to see how God could use such a tragic event as the stoning of Stephen to help spread the church. As a result of Stephen's stoning, a great persecution broke out against the church at Jerusalem, and all except the apostles were scattered throughout Judea and Samaria. As they went they preached the Word, which resulted in its being spread wherever they went.

PHILIP'S MINISTRY

Acts 8:4-40

PHILIP IN SAMARIA — Acts 8:4-25

Philip was one of the seven that we were introduced to who was responsible for the distribution of food (6:1-6). Now, however, as a result of the persecution, we see Philip preaching in the region of *Samaria*. Like Stephen, Philip could also perform miraculous signs (remember in 6:6 the apostles had laid their hands on him). As a result of his ministry, many people were converted to Christ, one of which was a sorcerer named Simon.

Up to this point Christianity was simply an extension of Judaism. But with the Samaritan (who were half-breeds, half Jew and half Gentile) conversions things were beginning to change. To check out this situation, the apostles sent Peter and John (the top leaders of the Jerusalem church) to Samaria. They confirmed the work, prayed for them that they might receive the Holy Spirit, and placed their hands on them. At this, the Bible says that "they received the Holy Spirit".

The question here arises: What does it mean, "they received the Holy Spirit?" Was it the indwelling of the Holy Spirit for salvation, or was it the physical manifestations of the Spirit which God used to "kick-off" the Church? If their conversion recorded in verse 12 was an honest conversion, then we must assume that they received the Holy Spirit at this time (look back at Acts 2:38). We are not sure what these people did when they "received the Holy Spirit" (v. 17), but we do know that some type of physical manifestation took place, because the sorcerer Simon "saw" (8:18) that the Spirit was given at the laying on of the apostles' hands, and he wanted to buy this power. So. . . it was not the reception of the Holy Spirit for salvation, but it was the reception of the manifestations of the Spirit; God's "seal of approval" that the half-breed Samaritans could be admitted into the Church. Remember also that there is no record of Stephen and Philip performing miraculous signs until after the apostles had laid their hands on them (6:6).

PHILIP AND THE ETHIOPIAN — Acts 8:26-40

Philip, still being led by the Spirit, came in contact with the treasurer of the Ethiopians. This man was in his chariot reading from the fifty-third chapter of Isaiah (possibly the #l Messianic prophecy in the Old Testament). From this passage Philip led him to the good news about Jesus. As they traveled along the road, they came to some water and the Ethiopian said, "Look, here is water. Why shouldn't I be baptized?" He stopped the chariot, and they both went down into the water and Philip baptized him. It is most likely that this man went on to introduce the gospel to Africa. The gospel was slowly making its way "to the ends of the earth".

SAUL'S CONVERSION

Acts 9:1-31

This Saul had been one of the persecutors of the Church in Jerusalem. After giving approval to Stephen's death he began to destroy the Church. Going from house to house, he dragged off men and women and put them in prison. But this was not enough! He wanted to persecute the Christians, wherever they might be. So he got approval to go to Damascus to find Christians and take them as prisoners to Jerusalem.

As he traveled to Damascus, suddenly a light from Heaven flashed around him. He fell to the ground blind, and heard a voice say to him, "Saul, Saul, why do you persecute Me?" Saul asked, "Who are you, Lord?" Jesus then told him who He was and told him to go to Damascus and wait for further instructions, which he did.

At this time the Lord prepared a man in Damascus to minister to Saul. His name was Ananias. He questioned whether or not he should minister to Saul. At this the Lord said, "This man is my chosen instrument to carry My name before the Gentiles and their kings and before the people of Israel." So he went to the home where Saul was staying, laid his hands on Saul so he could regain his sight, and baptized him.

Combining the account in the first chapter of Galatians with that in the ninth of Acts, we learn that he immediately began preaching at Damascus; went for three years to Arabia; returned to Damascus only to face such a storm of persecution as he himself had formerly raised; escaped to Jerusalem, where he was introduced to the distrustful disciples by Barnabas; preached boldly in Jerusalem till a plot of the Jews and a vision from God (22:17-21) sent him to his native Tarsus.

PETER'S MINISTRY
Acts 9:32–12:25

IN LYDDA & JOPPA — Acts 9:32-43

As Peter traveled around the country, he went to visit the saints in Lydda. Here he healed a paralytic named Aeneas, which brought many people to the Lord. While there, Peter heard of a benevolent disciple in Joppa, named Dorcas, who had died. So, he went to Joppa and raised her from the dead. The result, again, was that many people believed in the Lord.

CORNELIUS — Acts 10:1-11:18

At Caesarea there was a Roman centurion who was devout and God-fearing. Although he was very religious, he was not a saved man. One day he had a vision. He was told to send for Peter, which he immediately did. Meanwhile Peter also had a vision. In it he saw Heaven opened and something like a large sheet being let down to earth by its four corners. It was full of all kinds of "unclean" animals (which the Jews had been commanded not to eat in the Old Testament). He was told, "Get up, Peter. Kill and eat." To which he replied, "Surely not, Lord! I have never eaten anything impure or unclean." The voice spoke to him a second time, "Do not call anything impure that God has made clean." This happened three times.

While Peter was still wondering about the meaning of the vision, the men sent by Cornelius arrived at the home where he was staying. At this the Spirit told Peter to go with them.

On the following day Peter arrived in Caesarea at Cornelius' home. You can imagine his thoughts as he traveled. Cornelius was a Gentile. What was God doing? And what about the vision? Cornelius called together his relatives and close friends to hear Peter's message. Peter said, "You are well aware that it is against our law for a Jew to associate with a Gentile or visit him. But God has shown me that I should not call any man impure or unclean." Then, after hearing about Cornelius' vision, he began to preach Jesus to them. His main point was Christ's death and resurrection.

While Peter was still preaching to them, the Holy Spirit came "*on*" all who heard the message. This is the second "Holy Spirit baptism" that we spoke of back on page 43. Again, we see it as a "seal of approval" from God. The Gentiles really can be a part of the church. So Peter said, "Can anyone keep these people from being baptized with water? They have received the Holy Spirit just as we have" (outward manifestations). So he ordered that they be baptized in the name of Jesus Christ.

Boy, what a stir this created in Jerusalem! Could Gentiles become Christians? They weren't circumcised! They didn't accept the law! This was the thinking of the orthodox Jew who had become a Christian. Their thinking was that a person must first become a Jew to become a Christian. But Peter had learned otherwise. When he was questioned he simply related the whole story to those in attendance. He said, "As I began to speak, the Holy Spirit came "*on*" them as He had come "on" us at the beginning. Then I remembered what the Lord had said, 'John baptized with water, but you will be baptized with the Holy Spirit.' So if God gave them the same gift as He gave us, who believed in the Lord Jesus Christ, who was I to think that I could oppose God."

When they heard this, they had no further objections and praised God, saying, "So then, God has even granted the Gentiles repentance unto life."

THE CHURCH IN ANTIOCH — Acts 11:19-30

Some of the disciples who had been scattered during the persecution after Stephen's death went to Antioch and preached to the Gentiles. Many believed and turned to the Lord. When news of this reached Jerusalem they sent Barnabas to Antioch to check it out. When he arrived and saw the evidence of the grace of God, he was glad and encouraged them all to remain true to the Lord with all their hearts, and a great number of people were brought to the Lord. It was also at this time that Barnabas went to Tarsus, found Saul, brought him to Antioch, and ministered with him for a year in Antioch. This passage also points out that the disciples were first called Christians at Antioch.

PETER'S ESCAPE FROM PRISON — Acts 12:1-19

It was about this time that King Herod (grandson of Herod the Great who was ruling at the time of Christ's birth) arrested some who belonged to the church, intending to persecute them. He had James, the brother of John, put to death. When he saw that this pleased the

Jews, he proceeded to arrest Peter also. He put him in prison, where he was guarded by 16 soldiers. But the church was earnestly praying for him.

The night before Herod was to bring Peter to trial, suddenly Peter was awakened by an angel. The chains miraculously fell off of Peter's wrists, so he followed the angel out of the prison. He went to a home where many people were praying for him. At first the servant girl was so excited that she forgot to open the door for Peter. Finally, the door was opened; he entered and told them the story of his release.

HEROD'S DEATH — Acts 12:20-25

In working out a quarrel with the people of Tyre and Sidon, Herod delivered a public address to the people. When the people shouted that his voice was like that of a god, and he did not deny it, an angel of the Lord struck him down, and he was eaten by worms and died.

In contrast to the persecutor's miserable demise, the Word of God continued to increase and spread. Jerusalem had been reached! Judea had been reached! Samaria had been reached! Now the "ends of the earth" needed to be reached.

TO THE ENDS OF THE EARTH

INTRODUCTION

In chapter 13 we see a major change in the book of Acts. The first twelve chapters recorded the events of the spread of Christianity in Jerusalem, Judea, and Samaria. Now the third part of the Great Commission begins to be fulfilled, as the gospel is taken to the"ends of the earth". We also see other changes taking place. From now on the key person will be Paul, not Peter, and the key city will be Antioch, not Jerusalem.

It is exciting to see how God's Holy Spirit controls the spread of Christianity. He began the church in Acts 2 with many signs and wonders. He gave the disciples the courage to speak the Word of God boldly (4:31). He was involved in the teaching of Stephen (6:10), and Philip (8:29). He led Peter to Cornelius' home (10:19,20), and confirmed that Gentiles could be a part of the church (10:44). And now in chapter 13 we see the Spirit leading again as the gospel begins to be spread "to the ends of the earth".

THE FIRST MISSIONARIES

The church in Antioch was blessed with many excellent leaders. One day as they were worshiping the Lord and fasting, the Holy Spirit said, "Set apart for me Barnabas and Saul for the work to which I have called them". So after they had fasted and prayed, they placed their hands on them and sent them off. John Mark also traveled with them as their helper.

Their strategy in this and later journeys was to head for a large city, enter the synagogue, and there try to persuade Jews to accept Christ. Only after Jews reject them do they turn to Gentiles. Their goal was to establish a church in a city, and leave it capable of functioning on its own, then they would move on.

So . . . the first missionaries departed, and quite naturally they headed for Cyprus, the home of one of them (Barnabas).

ON CYPRUS — Acts 13:4-12

When they arrived at Salamis (on the eastern side of the island of Cyprus), they proclaimed the Word of God in the Jewish synagogues. No mention is given of their success. It just simply says that they traveled through the whole island until they came to Paphos (on the western side of the island). While here they were asked to speak to the proconsul, Sergius Paulus, an intelligent man. While doing so, a sorcerer named Elymas opposed them. Saul (who will be called Paul from this point on) turned to Elymas, rebuked him, and smote him with blindness. Paul remembered his own blindness for three days after his Damascus road experience, and perhaps he hoped that in the case of the sorcerer the temporary loss of physical sight might result in his spiritual eyes being opened to the true light. We do not know the outcome in his life, but we do know that Sergius Paulus was amazed, and accepted the message of Jesus.

An important transition takes place in this first step of the mission. Saul is now called Paul. It was common for Jews to have two names, one Hebrew, the other Greek. The use of Paul's Greek name from this point on and its use in all of his letters no doubt are another indication of the major thrust of his mission — the Gentile world. At the same time Paul took leadership in the mission. From this point on he is mentioned before Barnabas and becomes the principal spokesman.

IN PISIDIAN ANTIOCH — Acts 13:13-52

Leaving Cyprus the party crossed the Mediterranean to Perga where John Mark decided to leave and return to Jerusalem. No reason is given for his defection, though evidently Paul considered whatever reason it was an unjustified one (15:38).

The missionaries left the coast, climbed the Taurus mountains and arrived at a plateau 3,600 feet above sea level. Here they entered the province of Galatia and soon arrived at a city called Pisidian Antioch.

On the Sabbath they went as usual to the synagogue. After the reading from the scriptures the synagogue rulers asked Paul and Barnabas if they had an encouraging message to share. Boy, did they ever! Paul stood up and addressed the crowd. His message was quite reminiscent of the sermon of Stephen, which Paul had heard some fourteen years earlier. Paul begins with a basic Old Testament history lesson, beginning with the exodus, and covering such things as: the Promised Land, the period of Judges, Samuel, Saul, and David. He used the righteousness of David as a spring-board to Jesus. He told them: 1) the Savior Jesus was a descendant of David, 2) John was not the Christ, but the one to follow him was, 3) the rulers of Jerusalem killed Jesus, 4) but God raised Him from the dead, 5) and many people are witnesses of this fact, 6) it was prophecied in the scriptures, 7) and it is through Jesus that the forgiveness of sins is being proclaimed to you.

As Paul and Barnabas were leaving the synagogue, the people invited them to speak further about these things on the next Sabbath. When that day came almost the whole city gathered to hear the Word of the Lord. When the Jews saw this, they were jealous and talked abusively against what Paul was saying. So Paul and Barnabas boldly answered them,"We had to speak the Word of God to you first. Since you reject it and do not consider yourselves worthy of eternal life, we now turn to the Gentiles". Then they quoted Isaiah 49:6 to back up their position. The Gentiles, however, were glad, and honored the Word of the Lord, and believed. The Word of the Lord spread through the whole region. But the Jews stirred up persecution against Paul and Barnabas, and expelled them from their region.

IN ICONIUM — Acts 14:1-7

As usual they went to the Jewish synagogue. There they spoke so effectively that a great number of Jews and Gentiles believed. But the Jews who refused to believe stirred up the Gentiles and poisoned their minds against the brothers. Finally, Paul and Barnabas learned that there was a plot forming to kill them, so they moved on.

IN LYSTRA — Acts 14:8-20

It was here that Paul healed a man who had been lame from birth. When the crowd saw what Paul had done, they shouted in the Lycaonian language, "The gods have come down to us in human form!" Barnabas they called Zeus, and Paul they called Hermes because he was the chief speaker. They even prepared to make a sacrifice to Paul and Barnabas. When they realized what was happening, they tore their clothes and explained that they, too, were only men. Even with all their explaining, they had difficulty keeping the crowd from sacrificing to them.

Then some Jews came from Antioch and Iconium and won the crowd over. They stoned Paul and dragged him outside the city, thinking he was dead. What a quick reversal of these peoples' thinking! From worship to murder! However, the Lord was not through with Paul yet. As the disciples gathered around him, he got up and went back into the city. Then the next day they left for Derbe.

IN DERBE — Acts 14:21

There is only one verse given to the ministry in this city. It simply says that they preached the good news and won a large number of disciples.

THE RETURN TRIP — Acts 14:21-28

From Derbe they returned to Lystra, Iconium, and Antioch. What boldness and courage this must have taken, as they could be sure that persecution would await them. None is mentioned, however. It says that they strengthened the disciples and encouraged them to remain true to the faith. They also appointed elders in each church and, with prayer and fasting, committed them to the Lord.

From the region of Pisidia they traveled back to Perga, then to Attalia, and then sailed back to Antioch, where the trip had begun. On arriving there, they gathered the church together and reported all that God had done through them and how He had opened the door of faith to the Gentiles. They stayed there a long time with the disciples.

THE JERUSALEM COUNCIL

Some men came from Judea to Antioch and were teaching that the Gentiles must be circumcised, or they were not saved. Paul and Barnabas debated with them over the issue, and finally decided to go to Jerusalem to meet with the apostles and elders to settle the issue. When they arrived in Jerusalem they reported everything God had done through them. Then a Christian Pharisee stood up and said, "The Gentiles must be circumcised and required to obey the law of Moses". The question they then wrestled with was this, "Does a Gentile have to become a Jew before he can become a Christian?

After much discussion, Peter got up and addressed the crowd. He reminded them that God had sent Holy Spirit baptism upon Cornelius and his household, thus showing His acceptance of them. He concluded by saying, "We believe it is through the grace of our Lord Jesus that we are saved, just as they are".

After this Paul and Barnabas continued to tell about the miraculous signs and wonders God had done among the Gentiles. When they finished, James (the brother of Jesus, who was a leading elder in the Jerusalem church) spoke up. He backed up what Peter had said and continued by quoting Amos 9:11,12 as a prophecy of the salvation of the Gentiles. He concluded by saying, "It is my judgment, therefore, that we should not make it difficult for the Gentiles who are turning to God. Instead we should write to them, telling them to abstain from food polluted by idols, from sexual immorality, from the meat of strangled animals and from blood". These requests were to show the Jewish brothers that their side of the issue had been heard. They would allow for fellowship between Jewish and Gentile Christians to take place much more easily.

A LETTER TO GENTILE BELIEVERS — Acts 15:22-35

The church at Jerusalem thought that it was wise to send a letter to the Gentile believers explaining their decision. So, they drafted a letter and sent it with Paul and Barnabas. Also they chose two men who were leaders in the church to travel with Paul and Barnabas. Their names were Judas (called Barsabbas) and Silas. By sending them, the letter was given additional clout.

When they arrived in Antioch they gathered the church together and delivered the letter. The people read it and were glad for its encouraging message. Judas and Silas stayed there for some time, encouraging and strengthening the brothers. Then they headed home for Jerusalem.

LESSON #16

ACTS 15:36–21:14

TO THE ENDS OF THE EARTH — AT ANY COST!

INTRODUCTION
Acts 15:36-40

Paul and Barnabas had finished their first missionary journey, and had settled the issue in Jerusalem concerning whether or not the Gentiles had to first become Jews before they could become Christians. After spending some time in Antioch ministering to the people, Paul wanted to go visit the churches that they had established on their journey. Barnabas wanted to take John Mark along, but Paul did not because he had deserted them during their first trip (13:13). They had such a sharp disagreement that they parted company. Barnabas took Mark and sailed for Cyprus, but Paul chose Silas and went through Syria and Cilicia, strengthening the churches. It is good to know that Mark was later restored to Paul's confidence (2 Timothy 4:11).

Paul's initial purpose for the trip was to visit the churches that he had already established. In doing this they could personally deliver the decision reached by the apostles and elders in Jerusalem (15:23-29). But it won't take him long before he is spreading the Word to new areas.

PAUL'S SECOND MISSIONARY JOURNEY
Acts:15:41-18:22

At Lystra he found a young dtsciple named Timothy who was a very reputable young man. His father was a Greek, but he had been religiously raised by his Jewish mother, Eunice, and his grandmother, Lois (2 Timothy 1:5). He was evidently converted on Paul's first journey. Paul wanted to take Timothy along, but there was one problem. Timothy was not circumcised. So he circumcised him. Some have accused the apostle of inconsistency, especially since the Jerusalem council stated that circumcision was not necessary for salvation. But that was not the issue here. Paul's concern was not for Timothy's salvation. His concern was for the most effective possible communication of the gospel to both Jew and Greek! Uncircumcised, Timothy would be an offense to Jews, seen as one who had rejected their culture. Now he would be recognized as one who identified himself with their traditions, who belonged to them.

Notice how God's spirit is still leading their adventures. He kept them from preaching in Asia and Bithynia, because He had other plans for them. While in Troas Paul had a vision of a man of Macedonia begging him to come to Macedonia, so, Paul, concluding that the vision was from God, sailed for Macedonia.

It is at this point in the text that Luke, the writer, begins to use the words, "us", and "we". So . . . we conclude that this is when Luke joined Paul in his travels.

IN PHILIPPI — Acts 16:11-40

In Philippi we see no synagogue. Could it be that there were not even the ten Jewish men in the city that it took to form a synagogue? Could there be a current of anti-semitism in Philippi? Whatever the case may be the visiting preachers went outside the city on the Sabbath to the river, expecting to find a place of prayer. They shared Christ with the women present, and Lydia (a dealer in purple cloth — which signifies that she was probably quite wealthy) responded to the message and was baptized. She then persuaded the men to stay at her house.

While in Philippi the men were followed for days by a slave girl who had a spirit by which she predicted the future. She kept shouting, "These men are servants of the Most High God, who are telling you the way to be saved". Although she was telling the truth, it obviously annoyed the men. Finally Paul rebuked the spirit and told it to come out of her.

When the owners of the slave girl realized that their money maker was now silenced, they seized Paul and Silas and dragged them before the authorities. The whole crowd got involved so that the magistrates had them beaten and thrown into prison.

The pain and discomfort suffered by the two missionaries was terrible. Their backs were bruised if not raw from the beating. The stocks were not only used to hold the men, but were actually instruments of torture. By midnight their bodies throbbed with pain and they were no doubt hungry and thirsty as well, but they continued their witnessing task. They were praying and singing hymns to God. Suddenly there was a violent earthquake that opened the doors and loosed all of the prisoners' chains. When the jailer awoke he was about to kill himself (if any escaped he would be tried and killed, so why not get it over with?) when Paul shouted, "Don't harm yourself! We are all here!" The jailer was so shocked that he came trembling before the men and said, "What must I do to be saved?" (He was definitely affected by the praying and singing). The result was that he and his whole household believed and were baptized.

IN THESSALONICA — Acts 17:1-9

Here, as in most cities, Paul went to the synagogue on the Sabbath Day and reasoned with those present from the scriptures. He did this for three weeks. Many Jews, God-fearing Greeks, and not a few prominent women were persuaded and joined Paul and Silas.

The Jews, however, were so jealous that they formed a mob and started a riot in the city. That night Paul and Silas left for Berea.

IN BEREA — Acts 17:10-15

Now the Bereans were of more noble character than the Thessalonians, for they received the message with great eagerness and examined the scriptures every day to see if what Paul said was true. Many of the Jews believed as did also a number of prominent Greek women and many Greek men.

The Jews back in Thessalonica heard the reports from Berea. So they sent some men to Berea who agitated the crowds against Paul. Paul was sent away immediately, but Silas and Timothy stayed at Berea for some time.

IN ATHENS — Acts 17:16-34

Paul was basically waiting for Silas and Timothy in Athens. However, he could not miss out on such a great opportunity as this, so he reasoned in the synagogue and in the marketplace with those who would listen. After a dispute with some philosophers, he was brought to a meeting of the Areopagus (who had jurisdiction over moral questions and religious matters). While before these men Paul delivered the second of his addresses that have come down to us. Although it is quite different than his address to the Jews (13:16-41), the goal is the same — to preach the crucifixion and resurrection of Christ. When these men heard about the resurrection, some of them sneered, while others wanted to hear more. The result: a number of people believed Paul's message.

IN CORINTH — Acts 18:1-17

In Corinth Paul met some fellow tentmakers, Aquila and Priscilla. He stayed and worked with them for some time, reasoning in the synagogue each Sabbath Day.

Finally Silas and Timothy arrived from Macedonia. At this Paul devoted himself exclusively to preaching (it is probable that Silas and Timothy brought with them an offering from the Philippian church — see Philippians 4:15).

Again the Jews opposed him, so this time he shook out his clothes in protest and told them that he would go to the Gentiles. However, many Corinthians believed and were baptized, including the ruler of the synagogue, Crispus.

One night while in Corinth Paul received a very encouraging vision where the Lord told him that He was with him and that no one would harm him in the city. So Paul stayed there for a year and a half, teaching them the Word of God.

The Jews tried to defeat Paul by bringing him to court, but the procounsul, Gallio, wanted nothing to do with the problems concerning Jewish law, so he threw the case out of the court. Oh yes! When God speaks, He means it!

THE TRIP HOME — Acts 18:18-22

On Paul's trip back to Antioch he stopped at Ephesus where he went into the synagogue and reasoned with the Jews. They wanted him to stay, so he said that he would return, if it was God's will. From here he sailed to Caesarea, went to Jerusalem to greet the church, and then went to Antioch.

PAUL'S THIRD MISSIONARY JOURNEY
Acts 18:23-21:14

After spending some time in Antioch, Paul again set out to strengthen the churches.

Meanwhile, a Jew named Apollos, a learned man, with a thorough knowledge of scripture, began to preach in Ephesus. His only problem, however, was that he only knew about the baptism of John. So . . . Aquila and Priscilla (who were left in Ephesus by Paul) invited him to their home and explained to him the way of God more adequately. After this Apollos traveled to Achaia and enjoyed much success preaching the Word.

IN EPHESUS — Acts 19:1-20:1

Ephesus was the leading city of the seven provinces into which the great peninsula of Asia Minor was divided. Its geographical position on the important trade route between Rome and the Euphrates brought abundant commerce through its busy port. The temple to Diana (Artemis) was its crowning glory. It had been 220 years in building and was reckoned among the seven wonders of the world. Multitudes of pilgrims from all countries went there to worship. It contained a greatly revered image of the goddess which was believed to have fallen from heaven. This is the city in which Paul would minister for the next few years.

Upon arriving in Ephesus Paul asked some disciples if they had received the Holy Spirit when they believed. To his surprise they did not even know that there was a Holy Spirit. They told him that they had only received John's baptism. He explained that John's baptism and teaching was to lead people to Jesus. At this they were baptized into the name of the Lord Jesus (see 2:38). Then Paul placed his hands on them, and the Holy Spirit came "on" them so that they spoke in tongues and prophesied. Again, when the Holy Spirit came "on" someone it was not for salvation, but it was God's external "seal of approval" to show that what was happening was from God Himself.

For three months Paul taught in the synagogue. When opposition arose he moved to the lecture hall of Tyrannus, and taught for two years.

During his stay in Ephesus seven sons of the Jewish chief priest Sceva tried to cast out a demon in Jesus' name. The evil spirit said, "Jesus I know and Paul I know about, but who are you?" At this he jumped on the seven, and beat them until they ran from the house bleeding. The result was that the name of Jesus was highly esteemed. Many people confessed their sins and many brought together scrolls about sorcery and burned them. In this way the Word of the Lord spread widely and grew in power.

About this time a silversmith named Demetrius called together the workmen in related trades and got them stirred up over Paul's teaching and how it affected their pocketbooks (these men made idols, which Paul was preaching against). They became furious, seized a couple of Paul's companions and rushed into the theatre. For hours the people shouted, and caused a great confusion. Finally the city clerk calmed the crowd and quietly sent them away. After this, however, Paul sent for the disciples, encouraged them, said good-bye and set out for Macedonia.

THE TRIP TO JERUSALEM — Acts 20:2-21:14

Paul had already stated that he wanted to go to Jerusalem (19:21). He wanted to make a quick trip through Achaia and Macedonia first, however. After doing this Paul sailed to Troas. While there Paul spoke one evening all night long. At about midnight a young man named Eutychus fell asleep in a window and fell out of the third story window to his death. Paul went down, threw himself on the young man's body, and raised him to life again.

When they reached Miletus Paul sent for the Ephesian elders. Upon their arrival they spent intimate fellowship together, as Paul told them that they would never see him again. Paul spoke of the hardships ahead of him in Jerusalem. He said, "I consider my life worth nothing to me, if only I may finish the race and complete the task the Lord Jesus has given Me." He then went on to instruct the elders to "shepherd" the church — a wise thought for today's church leaders. When he was through speaking, they all knelt in prayer, and wept as they embraced him for the last time.

After many stops the ship finally landed at Caesarea. The men stayed at the home of Philip (cf. 8:4-40). While here Paul had an encounter with the prophet Agabus, who said that in Jerusalem Paul would be bound by the Jews and handed over to the Gentiles. Everyone present pleaded with Paul not to go to Jerusalem. Paul answered, "Why are you weeping and breaking my heart? I am ready not only to be bound, but also to die in Jerusalem for the name of the Lord Jesus". So, the people simply said, "The Lord's will be done."

PAUL — AND ME?

In everything that he did, Paul seemed to know the secret of contentment! What was this secret that would lead him through so much persecution: Jealously in Antioch (13:45), a plot to be stoned in Iconium (14:5), stoned in Lystra (14:19), beaten and thrown in prison at Philippi (16:23), a riot in Thessalonica (17:5), more agitation in Berea (17:13), accused of advocating foreign gods in Athens (17:18), abusive Jews in Corinth (18:6), and a riot in Ephesus (19:40). Paul gives us his secret in Philippians 4:11-13:

"I have learned to be *content* whatever the circumstances. I know what it is to have plenty I have learned the *secret* of being *content* in any and every situation, whether well fed or hungry, whether living in plenty or in want. *I can do everything through Him who gives me strength.*"

HOW ABOUT ME? Am I content that the Lord is currently taking care of every one of my needs?

REVIEW OF PAUL'S MISSIONARY JOURNEYS

JOURNEY	YEARS	KEY COMPANIONS	KEY CITIES	PASSAGES
1	2	Barnabas	Paphos Pisidian Antioch Iconium Lystra Derbe	13:-14:28
2	3	Silas Timothy Luke Aquila & Priscilla	Philippi Thessalonica Berea Athens Corinth	15:36-18:22
3	4	Timothy Erastus Sopater Aristarchus Secundus Tychicus Trophimus	Ephesus	18:23-21:14

ON TO ROME

INTRODUCTION

We recall from our last lesson that Paul wanted to go to Jerusalem, no matter what the outcome might be. He was even warned by his friends, a prophet, and the Holy Spirit that danger awaited him there. But on he continued, even willing to die in Jerusalem for Jesus.

PAUL'S IMPRISONMENT IN JERUSALEM
Acts 21:15-23:22

PAUL IS ARRESTED — Acts 21:15-22:30

When Paul arrived in Jerusalem he was warmly greeted by the church. However, on the outside there was resentment to Paul's ministry to the Gentiles by the Jews. One day while Paul was in the temple they grabbed him. Shouting all kinds of lies they stirred up the crowd against him and while they were trying to kill him the news reached the Roman commander, who quickly saved Paul's life. Since the commander could not figure out what was happening, he had Paul taken to prison. On the way Paul convinced the commander to let him speak to the crowd.

Paul simply gave his testimony. He told about his training under Gamaliel, about his zealousness for the law, and his persecution of Christianity. He then told of his miraculous conversion, and how the Lord was sending him to the Gentiles. When the Jews heard this, they caused an uproar against Paul. The commander then had Paul taken into the barracks, where he was about to have him flogged, until he learned that Paul was a Roman citizen.

BEFORE THE SANHEDRIN — Acts 22:30-23:22

The next day the commander had Paul brought before the Sanhedrin, to find out exactly why Paul was being accused by the Jews. When Paul realized that his defense would get nowhere with these men he stated that he was a Pharisee who was being tried because of his hope in the resurrection, which caused a great dispute between the Pharisees and Sadducees (the Sadducees believed that there was no resurrection, or angels, or spirits, where the Pharisees believed in all of these things). Finally the commander was afraid for Paul's life, and had him taken back to the barracks.

The following night the Lord stood near Paul and said, "Take courage! As you have testified about Me in Jerusalem, so you must also testify in Rome." So here we have a hint that somehow through all of this persecution the Lord was going to get Paul to Rome.

The next day the Jews formed a conspiracy to kill Paul. When their plot was found out, the commander sent Paul at night to Caesarea.

PAUL'S IMPRISONMENT IN CAESAREA
Acts 23:23-26:32

THE TRIAL BEFORE FELIX — Acts 24:1-27

Five days later Ananias the High Priest, some of the elders, and a lawyer named Tertullus came to Caesarea to state their case against Paul to the governor, Felix. They told lie upon lie about Paul. They said that he was causing trouble everywhere he went, stirring up riots, and that he had desecrated the temple.

Finally it was Paul's turn. He simply pleaded his case. He told Felix the truth about what had happened in Jerusalem. He then told how he worshiped God as a follower of "The Way."

After more of Paul's case Felix adjourned the meeting and stated that he would decide the case when the Roman commander of Jerusalem came to Caesarea. However, two years passed with no decision. Many times during this period Felix would send for Paul, hoping to receive a bribe. Finally Felix was succeeded by Porcius Festus, but because Felix wanted to grant a favor to the Jews, he left Paul in prison. It should be noted that during this two years Felix allowed Paul some freedom and permitted his friends to take care of his needs.

THE TRIAL BEFORE FESTUS — Acts 25:1-12

When Festus arrived in the region he went up to Jerusalem. While there the Jewish leaders presented their charges against Paul, and asked that he be transferred to Jerusalem (for they wanted to kill him on the way). Festus said that when he went to Caesarea that he would try him, which is what happened. Again the Jews told many lies about Paul, to which he simply told Festus that he had done no wrong. Festus then asked Paul if he was willing to go to Jerusalem to stand trial. Paul could see right through this scheme, so he said, "I appeal to Caesar!" This right of appeal was a right of Roman citizens to have their case sent directly to Rome, to be tried by the emperor himself. After Festus had conferred with his council, he declared: "You have appealed to Caesar. To Caesar you will go!"

BEFORE AGRIPPA — Acts 25:13-32

During this time King Agrippa came to Caesarea to pay his respects to Festus. While he was there Festus explained Paul's case to him. Agrippa was interested enough to hear Paul's case himself (although it was not officially a trial, since Paul had already appealed to Caesar). Festus was also looking for something to write to Caesar about Paul.

Paul's speech to this large group of dignitaries was masterful. Paul showed great tact and courtesy, and yet he was also to the point about the truths of Christ. He appears to be speaking directly to the king as one who was an expert of the Jewish religion, and therefore would understand what he was talking about.

At one point Festus called Paul insane, but Paul kept appealing to Agrippa's vast knowledge of the Jews. Finally the dignitaries rose and left the room. They acknowledged that he had done nothing worthy of death, and that he could have been set free if he had not appealed to Caesar.

THE TRIP TO ROME
Acts 27:1-28:15

A Roman centurion named Julius, who belonged to the Imperial Regiment, was given charge over Paul and some other prisoners. They set sail from Caesarea and headed along the coast to the north towards Asia. At Myra in Lycia they found an Alexandrian ship sailing for Italy, which they boarded. The wind was rough so they sailed near Crete, and landed at Fair Havens. While here Paul warned them not to sail further because of the time of year. But the centurion and pilot decided to attempt to sail to a larger and safer port on Crete.

While attempting this a wind of hurricane force swept them out to sea. They took many safety precautions, including the throwing overboard of the cargo and the ship's tackle. After days of being thrown about by the wind and waves, the men had given up all hope of being saved.

It was at this time that Paul received a message from the Lord that they would all be spared. Finally on the fourteenth night they realized that they were near land. Before dawn Paul encouraged them and got them to eat some food. Finally at daybreak they decided to run the ship aground on a sandy beach. In attempting to do this the ship ran aground on a sandbar and began to break up. The soldiers planned to kill the prisoners, to keep them from escaping. But the centurion wanted to save Paul's life, so he kept them from carrying out their plan. Those who could swim did so, while others grabbed pieces of the ship and floated ashore.

Once on shore they discovered that it was the island of Malta, where they were treated kindly by the islanders. While there Paul healed many, including the father of Publius, the chief official of the island. When they were ready to sail, they were given the needed supplies.

Isn't it interesting to note that through this entire ordeal, Paul, a prisoner, had exercised the true leadership over the 276 people who were aboard the ship.

After three months on Malta they sailed for Rome. After a few stops along the way they finally landed at Puteoli, where from here they would walk the remaining distance to Rome. They stayed with some disciples at Puteoli for a week and then set out for Rome. On the way they were met by some believers in Rome who had come to greet Paul. They traveled over forty miles to greet him and travel with him to Rome. This reception encouraged him greatly.

AT ROME
Acts 28:16-31

When they reached Rome Paul was allowed to live by himself, in his own home. However, a guard was always to be with him. Paul's first mission was to meet with the Jews in Rome. When this occurred, he was pleased to hear that the evil reports from Jerusalem had not reached Rome. On the other hand they seemed very interested to hear him speak of Christianity. Many believed, but others did not. Finally Paul told them that he must preach to the Gentiles, because they would listen.

For two whole years Paul stayed there in his own rented house and welcomed all who came to see him. Boldly and without hindrance he preached the Kingdom of God and taught about the Lord Jesus Christ.

Here Luke ends his narrative. Various theories have been put forth to explain why he went no further. The simplest is that he had achieved his goal. He had shown how the gospel was taken from Jerusalem, the Jewish center, to Rome, the Gentile capital. He traced each step as the church grew from a sect within Judaism to the universal Body of Christ.

PAUL'S LATER YEARS

An early tradition states that Paul was acquitted at his first Roman trial; that he carried out his plan to take the gospel to Spain and then resumed his labors in Asia, Macedonia, and Greece. But later he was arrested and brought back to Rome. We have no reason to doubt the ancient tradition which says the apostle was finally beheaded in Rome on the orders of the emperor, Nero.

WHAT AN EXAMPLE!

Paul gives us an unparalled example of steadfast faith in Jesus. In 2 Corinthians 11:24-29 he lists the many persecutions that he endured. He said: "Five times I received from the Jews the forty lashes minus one. Three times I was beaten with rods, once I was stoned, three times I was shipwrecked, I spent a night and a day in the open sea, I have been constantly on the move. I have been in danger from rivers, in danger from bandits, in danger from my own countrymen, in danger from Gentiles; in danger in the city, in danger in the country, in danger at sea; and in danger from false brothers. I have labored and toiled and have often gone without sleep; I have known hunger and thirst and have often gone without food; I have been cold and naked. Besides everything else, I face daily the pressure of my concern for all the churches."

Take a few minutes and jot down a few thoughts that you have had as you've been able to relate your life to Paul's throughout the last few lessons.

ACTS — AN UNFINISHED BOOK!

We need to always remember that the book of Acts describes one important phase of the history of the church, but that history is far from complete. As we take the Good News to our family, neighbors, friends, and associates we are continuing with the mission begun in Acts. Thus, the book of Acts becomes for us a continual challenge to reach more and more people for Christ.

REVIEW AND INTRODUCTION TO THE LETTERS

REVIEW

Fill in the following "REVIEW" activities:

BeeP SLoWLy, JaKe CaRRieS CoCoa

THE STRUCTURE OF THE NEW TESTAMENT

( )

( )

( )

( )

( )

P
P
O
S
T

THE STRUCTURE OF "ACTS"

GEOGRAPHICAL MOVEMENT	CHAPTERS	KEY PERSONALITY

SCHEDULE FOR "OVERVIEW STUDY OF THE 'LETTERS' "

DATE	STUDY MATERIAL
9/21	Review and Introduction
9/21	Romans
9/21	1 & 2 Corinthians
10/12	Galatians, Ephesians, Philippians
10/19	Colossians, 1 & 2 Thessalonians
10/26	1 & 2 Timothy, Titus, Philemon
11/2	Hebrews & James
11/9	1 & 2 Peter, 1-3 John, Jude
11/16	Revelation & Review

CHRONOLOGICAL ORDER OF PAULINE LETTERS

Periods of Paul's Life	Letter	Approximate Date (A.D.)	Place of Writing
SECOND MISSIONARY JOURNEY (A.D. 48-51)			
	1 Thessalonians	50	Corinth
	2 Thessalonians	51	Corinth
THIRD MISSIONARY JOURNEY (A.D. 54-58)			
	1 Corinthians	54	Ephesus
	2 Corinthians	54	Macedonia
	Galatians	55	Macedonia
	Romans	56	Corinth
FIRST IMPRISONMENT (A.D. 58-63)			
	Colossians	61	Rome
	Ephesians	61	Rome
	Philemon	61	Rome
	Philippians	62	Rome
BETWEEN IMPRISONMENTS (A.D. 64-66)			
	1 Timothy	64-66	Macedonia
	Titus	64-66	?
SECOND IMPRISONMENT (A.D. 66-68)			
	2 Timothy	66-68	Rome

CHRONOLOGICAL ORDER OF GENERAL LETTERS

Letter	Author	Approximate Date (A.D.)	Place of Writing	Written to:
James	James, the brother of Jesus	45-48	?	The 12 tribes scattered among the nations
1 Peter	Peter	64-65	Rome ?	God's elect scattered throughout Pontus, Galatia, Cappadocia, Asia, & Bithynia.
2 Peter	Peter	66-67	?	Same as 1 Peter.
Hebrews	?	67-69	?	?
Jude	Jude, the brother of Jesus	75	?	Those who have been called.
1 John	John	85-90	Ephesus	?
2 John	John	85-90	Ephesus	The chosen lady and her children.
3 John	John	85-90	Ephesus	Gaius

REVIEW ACTIVITIES

Fill in each of the following "Review" activities:

P

B Y I T

P

P A K

N A M S

O

O B E D

F eW P eT S

L eT R oRy

S iT T

S

S P A T T

T

R A G G

	KEY WORD	WRITTEN TO WHOM	UNIQUENESS OF BOOK
MATTHEW			
MARK			
LUKE			
JOHN			
ACTS			

THE STRUCTURE OF THE NEW TESTAMENT

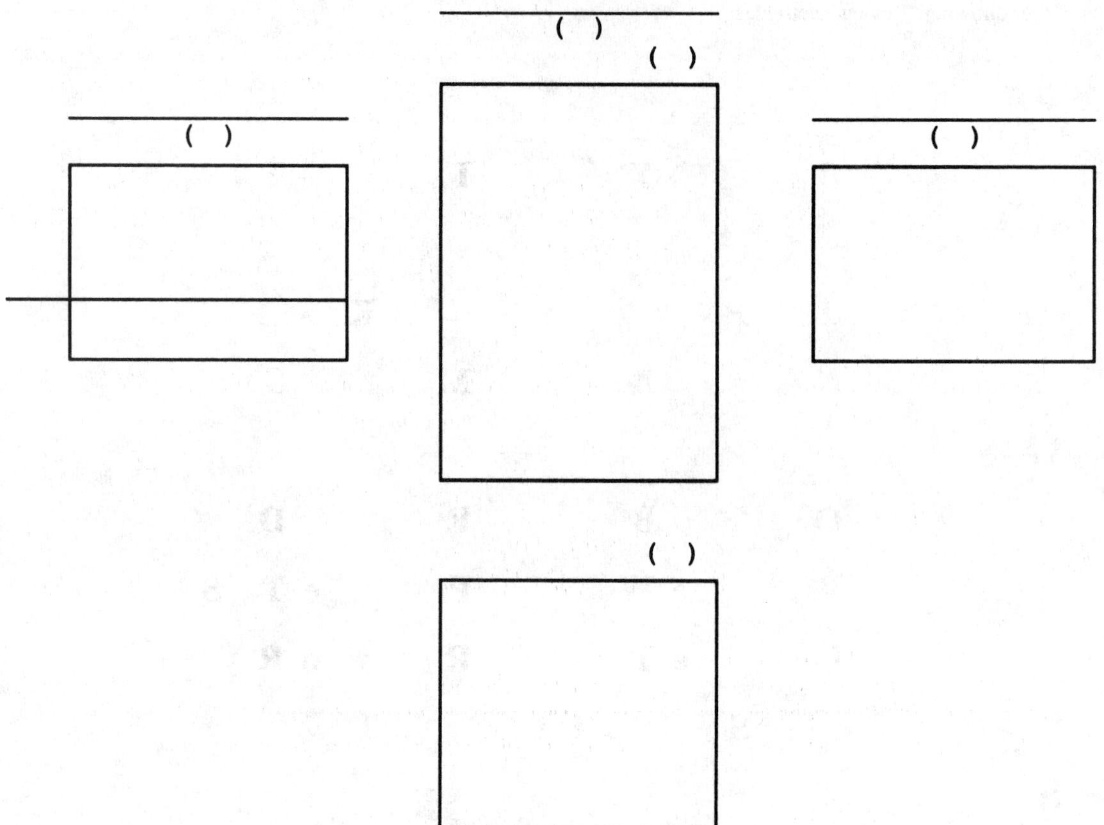

THE STRUCTURE OF "ACTS"

GEOGRAPHICAL MOVEMENT		CHAPTERS	KEY PERSONALITY

Quote Acts 1:8

LESSON #19

ROMANS

THE CHRISTIAN'S CONSTITUTION
KEY WORD: GOSPEL

The apostle Paul had longed for some time to go to Rome (1:13; cf. Acts 19:21). While in Corinth on his third missionary journey (approximately A.D. 56), before his departure to Jerusalem with the offering for the poor saints, he wrote this letter to the believers at Rome. It appears to have been delivered by Phoebe, a servant of the church at Cenchrea.

No one knows how the church began in Rome. It is quite possible that it began as Roman Jews returned to their city after the Day of Pentecost in Jerusalem (Acts 2). It may also be that converts of Paul, moving to the Imperial City from other provinces began the work of the church (notice in chapter 16 that Paul knows many of the Romans, yet he had never been there). Paul realized the importance of the church in the capital of the empire, so he longed to go there and strengthen the believers.

"Romans" was not Paul's first letter written to a church (see page 62), but it comes first in the section of the "Letters" because of its great importance. In it Paul covers a broad scope of Christian doctrine, ensuring that the Roman believers were basing their faith on the proper foundation. Many people have even called this book the "Constitution of Christianity."

INTRODUCTION — 1:1-17

What are the basic Christian truths laid out in Romans? After giving the greeting and expressing his longing to visit Rome, Paul sets forth his theme: *"I am not ashamed of the gospel because it is the power of God for salvation of everyone who believes, first for the Jew then for the Gentile. For in the gospel a righteousness from God is revealed, a righteousness that is by faith from first to last, just as it is written: 'The righteous will live by faith'* " (1:16,17). The rest of the letter, then, is an explanation of the *gospel* message.

THE GOSPEL NEED — 1:18-3:20

Paul moves quickly to establish the fact that all men are sinners. The Gentiles (1:18-32) are under God's wrath because although they had a knowledge of God's power and divinity through creation, they, through their sin, stifled this truth (1:18-20). Deliberately ignoring God they entered into idolatry (1:21-23). Finally God had to give them up because of their absolute moral degradation (1:24-32).

The Jews (2:1-3:20) also, long contemptuous of the Gentiles, convinced that Israel alone is God's chosen nation, are equally deserving of condemnation. They condemned others and practiced what they condemned (2:1). They felt that they would receive special treatment, simply because they were Jews (2:3). They misunderstood God's mercy as a license for sin and not an opportunity to repent (2:4). They boasted of their high standing of being the possessors of the Law, but all the while their lifestyle showed them to be no better than the Gentile (2:17-24). They also sought special attention because of circumcision, but, as Paul points out, even the uncircumcised can be regarded as circumcised through obedience to the Law (2:25-29). This is not to say that Jews have no advantage. They do, because God has entrusted His words to them, and God is faithful. The fault is not with God, not with the law, but with the sin of which Jews and Gentiles alike are guilty.

The result: "The wrath of God is being revealed from Heaven against *all* the godlessness and wickedness of men" (1:18). "There is *no one* righteous, not even One" (3:10). "*All have sinned* and fall short of the glory of God" (3:23). Therefore, God has already passed judgment on everyone — no matter how "good" they may think that they are and there is no chance of appeal. It is the decision of the Supreme Court of the Universe: "All have sinned." *Yes,* everyone has a need for the message of the Gospel.

THE GOSPEL PLAN — 3:21-11:36

Man cannot make it on his own, so God had to devise a plan: "Righteousness from God comes through *faith* in Jesus Christ to all who believe. There is no difference, for all have sinned and fall short of the glory of God, and are *justified freely* by His *grace* through the *redemption* that came by Christ Jesus" (3:22-24).

So . . . by God's grace (unmerited favor) toward us, He has justified (made righteous) us through our faith in Christ Jesus, who paid the penalty for our sin on the cross. The Judge will say, "Is there anyone to appear for the prisoners?" Then the Son of God says, "Yes, I am here to represent these. It is true that they committed these sins. It is true that they are guilty, but I bore their guilt on the cross. I died in their place that they might go free. I am their righteousness." And the Judge sets them free.

In the last analysis, man's standing before God depends not so much on what he has done, or can do, for himself, but on what Christ has already done for him. In chapter four Paul uses the example of the great Old Testament patriarch Abraham to show that a believer's righteousness does not come as a result of his or her own "works" to please God. "Abraham believed God, and it was credited to him as righteousness" (4:3).

In chapter five we have a comparison between Adam and Christ. Read 5:12-21 and write down words that describe Adam and the conditions that he brought to mankind, and other words that describe Christ, and the conditions that He brought to mankind.

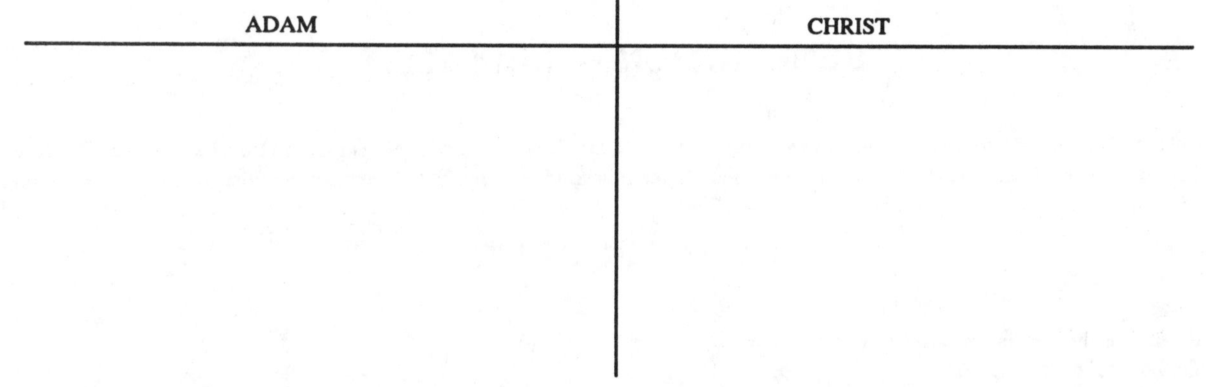

So . . . if one man's sin made it possible for all the race to die, then one man's righteousness made it possible for all of the race to get out of this condition.

Chapter six describes the believers relationship to sin. If we have been born again, then we cannot go on sinning in our old way (even though we may think we somehow get more grace that way), because we are no longer who we were. In our baptism we died and were buried. The person who arose from the watery grave is now united with Christ, alive to God and dead to sin. We used to be slaves of sin; now we are slaves of right living. We give ourselves over to what is holy, and as a result, we are going to live forever (6:23).

Paul also uses the example of marriage to make his point. As long as a couple is married, they are bound to each other. But if one dies, the other is free from the bond of loyalty to that person. Likewise, we died to sin when we became a Christian, and now are alive only to God through Christ.

Chapters seven and eight give us a great comparison between living under law (doing *my* best) and living by the Spirit. A quick glance at chapter seven will point out the over use of the word "I". Living under my own power only brings frustration and failure. Listen to the words of the man who tries to live by his own effort: "What a wretched man I am! Who will rescue me from this body of death?" (7:24).

Fortunately Paul does not leave us hanging. For in verse 25, and all of chapter eight he explains life "in Christ", lived under His direction and by His power. Finally "I" finds that there is One sufficient. Struggling yields to power, defeat is changed to victory, misery is transformed to joy. When "I" goes out, Christ comes in.

Chapter eight begins with the glorious truth. "Therefore, there is now no condemnation for those who are in Christ Jesus" (v. l), and goes on to discuss the life controlled by the Holy Spirit and the glory believers will experience in the future. It contains the promise of the Holy Spirit's help in prayer (see vv. 16,17), the famous assertion that "in all things God works for the good of those who love him, who have been called according to his purpose" (see v. 28), the less-often quoted statement of what that purpose is — "to be conformed to the likeness of his Son" — and the beloved promise that nothing can "separate us from the love of God that is in Christ Jesus our Lord" (vv. 29,39).

In chapters nine through eleven Paul discusses the situation of the nation Israel. If all of the blessings can be had through Christ, then what has happened to God's earlier covenant with Israel? Has God changed His mind? Not at all. He has remained faithful, but Israel has not! Had Israel believed and obeyed God and not rejected His authority, and had the Jews accepted Jesus as God's promised Savior, they would have been saved. But whoever chooses not to believe in Him cannot be saved.

God has not rejected His people. His people have rejected His Son. A new covenant has now succeeded the old, one that fulfills the intent of the old. What God promised Abraham, ("You shall become the father of a great nation") through faith in Jesus Christ He now has fulfilled. In Christ will all the true Israel of God be saved.

THE GOSPEL APPLIED — 12:1-15:13

The gospel of Jesus Christ is much more than a theological discussion (which Paul has given in chapters 1-11), it must be applied to our way of life. So here in chapter twelve Paul turns his thoughts toward Christian living. He had already told us that if we are living our lives controlled by God's Spirit, then we have an obligation to live by the Spirit (8:12). Here he tells us to offer our bodies as living sacrifices, and not to conform to the pattern of this world, but be transformed by the renewing of our minds (12:1,2). *NOW THIS IS CHRISTIAN LIVING!*

Paul then finishes this section of his letter by describing what it means to live by the Spirit. Humility, love, diligence, joyfulness, patience, prayerfulness, hospitality, and peacefulness are all results of the Spirit-filled life. Submitting to governing authorities, paying taxes, not being judgmental of other brothers and sisters, and not disputing over sacred days or what to eat is also part of Paul's encouragement to the Roman believers.

BENEDICTION — 15:14-16:27

In this section Paul again describes his own work as a minister to the Gentiles. He tells of his plans to travel to Spain and to stop by Rome on the way. He finally closes with a remarkable list of greetings to friends in a church he has never visited.

WHAT ABOUT ME?

Take serious thought as you answer these questions:
1) Do I need the Gospel? Why?

2) Have I accepted the message of the Gospel?

3) How is the Gospel daily transforming my lifestyle?

PAUL'S PROBLEM

The apostle Paul was ministering in Ephesus when he received reports that the church that he had established in Corinth years before was having a series of problems. Put yourself in his shoes and respond to these problems by filling in the chart below. Remember, Paul's goal was for these people to truly make Christ "Lord" of their lives.

Problem	How Would You Respond?
1. Certain people were causing divisions in the church.	
2. Immorality was commonplace.	
3. Christians were taking other Christians to court.	
4. Who should get married, and why?	
5. Should they eat meat sacrificed to idols?	
6. The Lord's Supper was being abused.	
7. People did not understand spiritual gifts.	
8. Some did not believe in the resurrection.	

CHURCH PROBLEMS IN A PAGAN SOCIETY
1 CORINTHIANS
KEY WORD: LORDSHIP

In Acts 18:1-11 Luke gives us the circumstances of the founding of the church at Corinth. This metropolis was the most splendid commercial city of Greece, strategically situated just south of the narrow isthmus connecting central Greece with the Peloponnesus. The city was the mecca of trade between the East and West. The city derived rich income from the transport of cargoes across the narrow isthmus.

As a port city Corinth was both wealthy and immoral. So depraved was the city that the term "to Corinthianize" was coined to denote the very practice of immorality. If ever the gospel had a place to prove its power (Rom. 1:16,17), it was at Corinth. It was therefore especially encouraging that "many of the Corinthians, hearing, believed and were baptized" (Acts 18:8). Therefore, it does not surprise us that on his Third Missionary Journey, during his stay at Ephesus, he was in constant contact with the church across the Aegean Sea. We know that to this congregation he sent a letter which, for some reason, has not come down to us (1 Cor. 5:9). At another time he personally visited Corinth (2 Cor. 12:14; 13:1).

It was toward the close of Paul's stay at Ephesus that those that were of the house of Chloe (1 Cor. l:11) reported to the apostle that the congregation at Corinth was being torn by strife. (It was all right for the church to be in Corinth, but it was fatal when Corinth got into the church.) He had also received a letter from the Corinthians themselves (7:1) filled with questions. So . . . he wrote this letter which we now call 1 Corinthians to deal with the sin that had arisen in the church. His constant theme is that Christ's Lordship must dominate in every area of individual and corporate living.

INTRODUCTION — 1 :1-9

Paul's greeting is full of grace and peace and thanksgiving for the church at Corinth. He also uses the word "Lord" six different times in these verses, preparing them for what was to come.

DIVISIONS — 1:10 - 4:21

Corinth was a very large city, with many congregations throughout, not just one big church as we might think. These, it seems, were developing into rival, competing groups, rather than cooperating with one another. One group said, "I follow Paul", another said, "I follow Apollos", another, "I follow Cephas" (Peter), and still another, "I follow Christ", attempting to exclude the others.

Paul simply points out their foolishness by getting them to see that Christ was the only one to be crucified for them. Paul, Peter, and Apollos were all good men, but they simply planted the seed and watered it. God was the one to bring the increase.

IMMORTALITY — 5:1-13; 6:12-20

A man in the church had an immoral relationship with his father's wife. And the church was proud of it — thinking that they had much grace if they could tolerate such a situation. Paul tells them that they should have been full of grief, and they should "expel the wicked man from among them."

Others in the church were involved with prostitutes. So Paul says, "Do you not know that your bodies are members of Christ Himself? Shall I then take the members of Christ and unite them with a prostitute? NEVER! Do you not know that your body is a temple of the Holy Spirit, who is in you, whom you have received from God? You are not your own; you were bought at a price. Therefore honor God with your body."

LAWSUITS — 6:1-11

Some Christians were taking their brothers to pagan courts over disputes. Paul's response is, "Is it possible that there is nobody among you wise enough to judge a dispute between believers? And if not, then why not be wronged? Why not rather be cheated?" This is so much better than disgracing the name of Christ in your community.

MARRIAGE — 7:1-40

Paul's wisdom on marital situations is as follows:

— If married, fulfill your marital duties (3)
— Do not separate from your spouse (10,ll)
— Those married to unbelievers, stay together and attempt to bring them to Christ (12-16)
— Unmarried, you can have more undivided devotion to Christ, but if you wish to marry — do so (32-38)
— You are committed to your spouse for life (39)

LIBERTY — 8:1–11:1

Should Christians eat meat that has been sacrificed to idols? Well . . . since idols are nothing at all, then this would be permissable, unless it made another stumble in his walk with the Lord. By using this illustration, plus whether or not he, Paul, should take a salary for his ministerial work, Paul discusses a Christian's freedom.

The Scripture does not lay down little rules for our conduct and tell us just the things we ought to do or not do, but rather states principles which should guide the Christian's actions. Someone has well said that Christian liberty does not mean the right to do as we like, but rather the right to do as we ought. Paul puts it, "Everything is permissible — but not everything is beneficial" (10:23). Yes, I can do anything I want to, but I must be sure my desires are to please Christ. What I do is an example to others, and may harm or bless them. I should not only answer the question, "Does my action harm weaker Christians?" but "Does it glorify God?"

ABUSING WORSHIP — 11:2–14:40

Paul has been arguing against eating meat offered to idols or claiming one's salary as a minister, not because it is wrong, but because it might be misunderstood. Now he applies the same reasoning to the question of women's freedom in worship. Since in the Lord men and women are not independent of each other, let them relate to one another in worship as seems proper.

Some were abusing the Lord's Supper. Along with what we today call the "Lord's Supper" they had a "Love Feast" which was a complete meal which accompanied the Lord's Supper. Many people would begin to eat as soon as they arrived, so that the result was that some remained hungry while others got drunk. Paul severely rebukes them and gives them clear instructions concerning the Lord's Supper in 11:23-29.

A large part of this section in the letter is concerned with the problem of spiritual gifts. Paul makes several points very clear as he deals with this situation: l) the gifts are manifestations of the Holy Spirit in the believer (12:4-11); 2) they are to be exercised in a spirit of love (13:1-13); 3) three gifts were to be in operation only until the New Testament was complete (13:8-13); and 4) things are to be done "decently and in order" (14:40). The sovereignty and lordship of God in the Church is emphasized in this passage. He has placed the members in the Body "just as He wanted them to be"(12:18), and each member is subject to Him as well as to every other member. Only as the members serve in this way can the Body be assured of proper operation. Strife, jealousy and envy will not advance but only deter the well-being of the whole organism.

THE RESURRECTION — 15:1-58

No doubt there was a group in the church who did not believe in the resurrection of the dead. Paul says, in effect, if we deny the resurrection, we deny one of the greatest of all truths of the Gospel. But more than all that, no resurrection would mean no Gospel at all, for we would be worshiping a dead Christ. There would be no "good news," for there would be no proof that God had accepted Christ's death as an atonement for our sins.

BENEDICTION — 16:1-24

We find Paul's conclusion in chapter sixteen. He makes plans, and gives final exhortations and greetings. It is quite evident that he loves these people greatly, even with their sin.

PAUL'S APOSTLESHIP IS DEFENDED

2 CORINTHIANS

KEY WORD: PAUL'S DEFENSE

Paul was somewhat worried as to how the church at Corinth would receive his first letter. He wondered how they had accepted his rebukes, so he sent Titus, and perhaps Timothy, to Corinth to find out the effect of his letter. During Paul's third missionary journey, while he was in Macedonia, Titus reported that the majority of the church had received the letter in the proper spirit. But there were those who doubted his motives, and even denied his apostleship, saying that he did not have the proper credentials for an apostle. Perhaps they questioned this because he was not one of the original Twelve. These enemies were bitter and tried to undermine him and his authority.

Accordingly, from Macedonia (Philippi?) Paul now writes 2 Corinthians. His purpose was threefold: (a) to express his gratitude for the manner in which the church, as a whole, had taken to heart the contents of 1 Corinthians; (b) to urge that the collection for the needy saints in Judea be carried forward energetically; and (c) to defend himself against the false charges which had been made by his enemies.

PAUL'S CHARACTER — CHAPTERS 1-7

Paul presents here a magnificent portrait of the glory of Christian ministry, and illustrates the effectiveness of personal integrity and testimony in service for Christ. Suffering, as Paul says, is a part of ministry, but God is always faithful. In this Paul is exposing his own character, and giving the Corinthians an example to follow.

This section is intertwined with personal messages and a defense of the message that Paul preached. Throughout these writings one can see straight in to the heart of Paul, his joys all the way down to his sorrows. One common emphasis of this entire section is the work of God on behalf of believers. God comforts (1:3,4; 7:6), delivers (1 :10), establishes (1:21,22), gives victory (2:14), enables (3:6), enlightens (4:6), empowers (4:7), resurrects (4:14), prepares (5:5), reconciles (5:18), beseeches (5:20) and receives as a Father (6:17,18).

The Corinthians may still have been troubled with moral laxity, because in chapters 5, 6 and 7 Paul warned them to avoid wordly friends. He concludes this first section by expressing his joy at their true repentance (see 7:2-16). The Apostle must have felt that he was getting somewhere with them.

PAUL'S COLLECTION — CHAPTERS 8 & 9

Using the Macedonia churches as an example and reminding the Corinthians of their former willingness, Paul urges them to give liberally for the needs of the poor brothers in Jerusalem and throughout Judea.

They were to give cheerfully, willingly, and generously, even if they too were poor. They were not expected to give because they had been commanded to do so, but because they had considered the example of Jesus and wanted to prove their love for Him. And God would take their gift and turn it into prayers of thanksgiving, blessing them abundantly, and meeting each of their personal needs.

These two chapters give us so much teaching on Christian giving that they have rightly been entitled by some as the "Philosophy of Christian Giving."

PAUL'S CREDENTIALS — CHAPTERS 10–13

Paul concludes his letter with a defense of his apostolic authority and credentials. He is directing his thoughts to the rebellious minority in the Corinthian church, who, it appears, are comparing Paul to their own set of standards and not to God's set of standards given to us in Christ (10:12-18).

To demonstrate his credentials, Paul is forced to boast about his knowledge, integrity, accomplishments, sufferings, visions, and miracles (11:l-12:13). But, Paul does not feel comfortable in talking so much about himself. Over and over again he says, "I am speaking as a fool" (11:1,17,21). His self-consciousness is part of the letter's appeal, however, exposing the very human side of this complex man. He suffers, he hurts, he cares, he cries, he gives everything he has for his ministry. He anguishes over the charges of his critics and over the damage they are doing to his beloved church. He does not write as an authoritative apostle so much as the spiritual father of these young Christians in Corinth whom he loves and wants to be loved by.

He reveals his plans to visit them for the third time and urges them to repent so that he will not have to use severity when he comes (12:14-13:10). The letter ends with an exhortation, greetings, and a beautiful benediction which includes the Father, Son, and Holy Spirit.

LESSON #21

GALATIANS–PHILIPPIANS

THE CHRISTIAN'S DECLARATION OF INDEPENDENCE

GALATIANS

KEY WORD: FREEDOM VERSUS SLAVERY

Paul's work in Galatia (especially Antioch, Iconium, Lystra, and Derbe) had been quite successful. In fact, great multitudes had become Christians. Sometime after Paul had left Galatia, certain Jewish Christians came along insisting that Gentiles could not be Christians without keeping the Law of Moses. These "Judaizers" were teaching a mixture of Judaism and Christianity, based on the false premise that Christianity could operate only within the sphere of the Mosaic Law.

The Galatians, it appears, accepted this teaching with the same wholeheartedness with which they had at first received Paul's message, and Paul could not stand this! After investing everything that he had, and even more, while preaching of the Gospel of Grace, to hear that they were digressing to belief in the law for justification really bothered Paul. The Apostle's purpose, therefore, in writing this letter was to refute the false teachings, and establish in the minds of his converts the true Gospel — that "A man is not justified by observing the law, but by faith in Jesus Christ" (2:16).

PAUL DEFENDS HIS AUTHORITY — 1:1-2:21

It appears that the Judaizers must have spread lies about Paul's authority as an apostle, because Paul begins the letter reminding the people of his own personal credentials. He makes it clear that he did not receive his message from man, but by direct "revelation from Jesus Christ" (1:12). Later Paul was confirmed by the leaders of the Jerusalem church (James, Peter, and John), who gave him the "right hand of fellowship" (2:9). Paul also tells of the profound effect that the gospel had on his own life. The fact that he had been "crucified with Christ, and lived only by faith in the Son of God" (2:20). These people knew that this was true, so it had to make an impact in their lives.

PAUL DEFENDS HIS MESSAGE — 3:1-4:31

These two chapters were written to defend the message of justification by faith to refute the false teaching of justification by works of the law.

Here Paul uses eight arguments against this false teaching:

1) Was the Spirit's work manifested among you because of your faith, or because you observed the law? So . . . why switch systems? (3:1-5).
2) Abraham "believed God, and it was credited to him as righteousness". The same is true today (3:6-9).
3) Scripture teaches that law brings a curse. But Christ brings the promise of the Spirit (3:10-14).
4) The promises made to Abraham were not based on the law (3:15-18).
5) The law was given to point out sin and to lead us to Christ (3:19).
6) Those who have been clothed with Christ through baptism are "sons", and "heirs", not slaves (3:26-4:7).
7) Oh, Galatians, how could you turn back to those miserable principles? (4:8-20).
8) The Abrahamic covenant brings freedom, where the Mosaic covenant brings slavery (4:21-31).

THE MESSAGE APPLIED — 5:1-6:18

Again Paul closes his letter with thoughts of applying the message that he had just delivered. "It is for freedom that Christ has set us free". Paul couldn't imagine how anyone could go back to a system of bondage (the law) after they had truly been set free by Christ. He explains that freedom from law does not mean lawlessness, but responsible living. The Christian is also free from the bonds of sin because of the indwelling Holy Spirit. Freedom gives us no excuse to indulge in the deeds of the flesh. Rather, it provides the privilege of bearing the fruit of the Spirit by putting total dependence in Him.

This letter closes with a contrast between the Judaizers, who are motivated by pride and a desire to avoid persecution, and Paul, who had suffered for the true gospel, but boasts only in Christ (6:11-18).

THE UNITY IN CHRIST'S CHURCH

EPHESIANS

KEY WORD: IN CHRIST

This is one of the four "prison letters", written during Paul's first Roman imprisonment. It is quite possible that this letter was sent as a circular letter, intended for distribution to all of the major churches of Asia Minor. It was not written to correct specific problems in a local church, but to prevent problems in the church universal by encouraging believers to base their philosophy of life on the great wealth of blessings that God had given them "in Christ".

GOD'S GIFTS — 1:1-3:21

"Praise be to the God and Father of our Lord Jesus Christ, who has blessed us in the heavenly realms with every spiritual blessing in Christ" (1:3). Paul moves from this statement to a listing of these blessings: We're adopted as His sons, we have redemption and forgiveness of sins, and we're sealed in Him with the promised Holy Spirit. Notice the work of the Trinity here. The Father adopts us, the Son redeems us, and the Holy Spirit seals us (1:3-14).

Next Paul shares a prayer that he continually prays for these people — namely that they would be enlightened to know the riches of God's grace and power which has been made available to them (1:15-23).

In chapter three, Paul describes the power of God's grace by contrasting their former condition with their present spiritual life in Christ, a salvation attained not by human works but by divine grace (2:1-10). This redemption includes Jews, yet also extends to those Gentiles who previously were "foreigners to the covenants of the promise" (2:12). In Christ, the two for the first time have become members of one body (2:11-22).

Again Paul prays for these believers. This time he goes a step further than his first prayer, where he prayed for their enlightenment. Here he prays for them to experience God's riches of power and love (3:14-21).

OUR RESPONSE — 4:1-6:24

Drawing upon the huge inheritance described in chapters one through three Paul now urges the Ephesians to "live a life worthy of the calling you have received" (4:1). This is what we call "transformed living". This involves the use of spiritual gifts in love (4:11-16), the putting off of the old self and putting on the new (4:20-24), imitating God (5:1), living a life of love (5:2), and submitting to one another out of reverence for Christ (5:21).

Paul then instructs these believers to walk "in Christ" in regards to every one of their social relationships also. He speaks to wives, husbands, children, fathers, slaves and masters (5:22-6:9).

Finally Paul points out that the Christian life includes warfare, but Christ is sufficient! Putting on His armor gives us the ability to have victory over the schemes of Satan (6:10-24).

THE LETTER OF JOY

PHILIPPIANS

KEY WORD: JOY

The church at Philippi, never slow in the business of sending gifts to help Paul in his need (Phil. 4:16), had heard about the apostle's imprisonment and decided to send him another gift. It is delivered by Epaphroditus, who may have been the pastor of the congregation. Paul, pleased with their genuine, Christlike spirit, writes to them, not because of any crisis, but to express his affection for them, his gratitude for their gift, his encouragement concerning their Christian growth, his admonitions against false teaching, and his thoughts about his circumstances.

The Epistle to the Philippians is one of the most intimate and personal of Paul's letters. It is filled with tender affection and joy. Its theme is the joy of knowing Christ, the concept of rejoicing occurring no less than sixteen times in the letter. The church at Philippi in Macedonia was the first assembly established by Paul in Europe. It was in a sense his best-loved congregation, for it entered more sympathetically into his sufferings and needs than any other church (4:14-20).

CHRIST OUR LIFE — 1:1-30

After a beautiful greeting of thanksgiving for the Philippian believers, he shares with them his joy that his chains are furthering the kingdom. He says, "Christ is preached, and because of this I rejoice" (1:18). He then goes on to explain that he would actually desire death, so that he could be with Christ, but he knew that he would live so that he could continue encouraging the brothers. His attitude was, "For to me, to live is Christ and to die is gain" (1:21). Paul also encouraged the Philippians to, "conduct yourselves in a manner worthy of the gospel of Christ" (1:27), especially in the face of inevitable coming suffering.

CHRIST OUR EXAMPLE — 2:1-30

Paul wants this church to be unified in Christ; to be "like-minded, having the same love, being one in spirit and purpose" (2:2). The secret to this unity is simply in adopting Christ's attitude. He knew what it meant to be God, and yet He gave it up in order to become a man and die for the salvation of mankind. What humility!

CHRIST OUR GOAL — 3:1-21

He begins this section by again refuting the teachings of the Judaizers. He says that all of his boasting in the flesh is mere trash when compared to the surpassing greatness of knowing Christ Jesus. This is his simple goal, which he continually strives to achieve.

CHRIST: OUR SUFFICIENCY — 4:1-23

Remember, Paul is a prisoner, and before this he had gone through many different types of sufferings for Christ's sake. But when it comes down to it, Paul can say, "I have learned the secret of being content in any and every situation, whether well fed or hungry, whether living in plenty or in want. I can do everything through Him who gives me strength" (4:12-13)

This joyous letter from prison closes with greetings and a benediction (4:21-23).

DEFENDING CHRIST'S SUPREMACY

COLOSSIANS

KEY WORD: CHRIST IS SUFFICIENT

Among Paul's letters, only "Romans" and "Colossians" were written to churches which had not been established by Paul himself. It is most possible that the church was a result of Paul's three-year ministry in Ephesus, as Colossae was about 100 miles east of Ephesus. It is also most possible that Epaphras was its founder (1:7).

"Colossians" is another letter which was written because of a problem in a local church. You see, many different false teachings were all creeping into the church at the same time. These false teachings comprise what we call today the "Colossian heresy." Paul's strategy to refute these teachings was not to argue each one down in a detailed debate. Instead, he simply showed the *sufficiency* and *supremacy* of Christ in all things.

INFORMATION — CHAPTERS 1 & 2

After Paul's greeting, thanksgiving, and beautiful prayer for the Colossians' spiritual growth, Paul gets right to the point . . . defending Christ's supremacy against the "Colossian heresy."

The "Colossian heresy" seems to be a mixture of Greek speculation, Jewish legalism, and oriental mysticism. Most certainly it embraced some of the basic ideas of what later came to be known as "Gnosticism." It involved: 1) A belief in human tradition (2:8), 2) Legalistic rule keeping (2:16), 3) Worship of angels (2:18), & 4) Asceticism (2:20-23). Each of these teachings was attempting to become an essential element of the gospel message in Colossae.

Paul's response to this heresy was to first simply show Christ's supremacy over all things, then to compare His supremacy to each specific heresy.

Read 1:15-20 and list the attributes of Christ mentioned in this passage.

Paul says that: 1) Those who believe in human tradition do so rather than believing on Christ (2:8), 2) Those that are legalistic don't realize that their rules were only a shadow of the reality, which is Christ (2:17), 3) Those who worship angels have lost connection with the Head, Christ (2:19), and 4) Those that believe that asceticism is the way to spirituality don't realize that these are mere human commands and teachings (2:22). Christ is indeed supreme over everything (1:18).

TRANSFORMATION — CHAPTERS 3 & 4

Paul not only wanted the Colossians to understand the implications of the sufficiency and supremacy of Christ to their belief system, but also to their lifestyle. So . . . chapters 3 and 4 are dedicated to this purpose. Because of his death with Christ, Paul states, the Christian must regard himself as dead to the old sinful self (3:5-9). And because of his resurrection with Christ, the Christian must regard himself as alive to Christ, which leads to virtues motivated by love (3:10-17).

He then gives further instructions to wives, husbands, children, fathers, slaves and masters. Finally he closes the letter by referring to specific friends in the ministry, and their usefulness to him.

THE SECOND COMING OF CHRIST
1 THESSALONIANS
KEY WORD: COMFORT IN CHRIST'S RETURN"

Thessalonica was a strategic city in the first century. It was the chief seaport of the region, and was also the capital of the Roman province of Macedonia. It was located on the main road from Rome to the east. This strategic location assured it of commercial success, but, as we have seen with other cities, like Corinth, this success also brought much immorality with it.

Paul's work in Thessalonica was during his second missionary journey, as recorded in Acts 17:1-10. Although he did not stay there long, he had great success, especially among the Gentiles. The Jews became jealous of Paul's success and organized a mob to oppose the Christian missionaries. As a result, they fled the city for Berea. The Jews from Thessalonica also drove them from Berea, so they headed to Athens. While here Paul sent Timothy back to Thessalonica to see how the believers were doing (1 Thessalonians 3:1,2). Then he moved on to Corinth. Timothy brought back good news when he returned to Paul at Corinth (Acts 18:5; 1 Thessalonians 3:6). So . . . Paul quickly writes this letter to encourage the church to keep walking in the way of the Lord. He also encouraged them in practical areas of Christian obedience.

THANKSGIVING — 1:1-10

After Paul's usual greeting of grace (Greek) and peace (Jewish), he gets right to telling these people how pleased he is with their faith. He says that through their suffering the Thessalonian church was a model to all the believers in Macedonia and Achaia, and that their faith was known everywhere.

PAUL'S MINISTRY — 2:1-3:13

It appears that in Thessalonica, as elsewhere, there was a group of people that were having problems with Paul, and his authority as an apostle. Accordingly, he responds to their attacks. Because God has entrusted him with the gospel (2:4), his message is a valid one. Both by words and by works his ministry has been exemplary (2:10). He reminds them how they received his message at the first as "the word of God" (2:13) and lived in the light of that standard. The message which Timothy brought to him of their endurance in affliction was a great comfort (3:6-8).

CHRISTIAN LIVING — 4:1-5:28

In a city such as Thessalonica Paul knows that immorality would continually be a temptation for the church. So he writes and simply tells them that they were not called of God to impurity, but holy living.

Paul also wants them to be knowledgable about Christ's Second Coming. It seems that the Thessalonians were worried about those that had already died, wondering if their departed brothers and sisters would miss out on the blessings to come. He comforted them with the teaching that those alive will have no advantage at the Second Coming over those that had already died. The dead in Christ will actually rise first, and those alive will join them to meet the Lord in the air. Paul also instructed that we do not know when the second coming will occur.

He then closes the book with some final teachings regarding their conduct with one another, reminding them that "the one who calls you is faithful and he will do it."

FURTHER TEACHING ON CHRIST'S SECOND COMING
2 THESSALONIANS
KEY WORD: WAIT PATIENTLY

Written just a short time after his first letter to Thessalonica, Paul wrote this letter to further clear up problem situations concerning the Lord's return.

THANKSGIVING — CHAPTER 1

Since Paul had left Thessalonica (cf. Acts 17:10), persecution had been the lot of the church. The attacks which had been directed first against the apostle were turned toward the believers there. Because of their endurance under the pressure of these onslaughts, Paul gave thanks to God for them. The day was coming, he assured them, when the Lord Jesus would be revealed from Heaven to take vengeance on all those "who know not God" (1:7,8). This was an encouragement for these people to persevere under persecution.

Paul also tells these people about how he boasts to other churches about their endurance under persecution. He then relates to them of his prayers for their spiritual maturity.

CHRIST'S SECOND COMING — CHAPTER 2

To clarify the wrong ideas which the Thessalonians had gotten about the coming of the Lord, whether from misunderstanding his first letter, from false teaching, from a forged letter (2:2), or from forgetting what he had taught them while he had been with them (2:5), the apostle in his second letter to them clearly teaches that the Lord's coming had not yet taken place. He says that it would not happen until the rebellion occurred and the man of lawlessness was revealed. There are many theories about the meaning of this teaching. The important thing to know is that the man of lawlessness is the one "whom the Lord Jesus will overthrow with the breath of his mouth and destroy by the splendor of his coming" (2:8).

WARNING AGAINST LAZINESS — CHAPTER 3

Paul begins this section asking for prayer for himself, and then encourages the Thessalonians by telling them that he was certain that they were obeying his commands.

However, there were those who were lazy. It seems that they were living off of the goodness of their brothers in the church. Paul simply says, "If a man will not work, he shall not eat" (3:10). What a motivation to get to work!

ADVICE FOR THE PASTOR AT EPHESUS

1 TIMOTHY

KEY WORD: CHURCH LEADERSHIP

Released from his first Roman imprisonment and apparently on his way to Asia Minor, Paul left Titus on the island of Crete to complete the organization of its churches (Tit. 1:5). At Ephesus the Apostle was joined by Timothy, who had evidently returned from Philippi (Phil. 2:19-23). Paul left for Macedonia, instructing Timothy to stay on at Ephesus in order to meet a great need there (1 Tim. 1:3,4). From Macedonia Paul wrote this First Letter to Timothy in Ephesus.

Timothy was a native of Lystra (Acts 16:1), and had been taught the scriptures since infancy (2 Tim. 3:15). He may have been converted on Paul's first trip through the area. During Paul's second missionary journey through this region, Paul heard such good reports about this young man that he decided to take him along in his travels. From this point on the two worked closely together in the establishment of churches.

The two letters to Timothy and one to Titus are often called Pastoral Epistles. These three short letters share a common theme: How to be a church pastor. From a veteran church leader to his younger apprentices, they are filled with practical instructions concerning the proper way to shepherd the flock of Christ.

Since 1 Timothy was written to Paul's close companion, he does not develop doctrinal themes, but assumes that these are already in place. Instead, he instructs the pastor of the Ephesian churches in practical areas of church life.

FALSE TEACHING - 1:3-11; 6:3-10

Paul had warned the church at Ephesus that savage wolves would come into the church and try to destroy it (Acts 20:29). Evidently this was taking place, as Paul begins his letter by instructing Timothy on how to handle this problem. The problem appears to be like the "Colossian heresy" studied in the last lesson. Paul says that these people promote controversies rather than God's work. Others taught that Godliness was the way to financial gain, so Paul points out that the love of money is a root of all kinds of evil (6:5-10).

PERSONALLY TO TIMOTHY 1:12-20; 3:14-6:2; 6:11-21

In these sections Paul is giving Timothy personal instructions in being a shepherd of God's flock. Paul uses his own example to give Timothy more strength to fight the good fight (1:12-20). He also exhorts Timothy to be an example in speech, in life, in love, in faith and in purity (4:12). Advice is given in the handling of widows, the paying of ministers, the teaching of slaves, and the attitudes of the rich.

WORSHIP 2:1-15

There appears to be a problem where some women were attempting to take control of the church. Paul informs them to learn in submission, and to adorn themselves with good deeds.

CHURCH LEADERSHIP 3:1-13

Here Paul lists qualifications for an overseer (elder, bishop) in the church. He must be above reproach in all of his dealings; at home, church, and in the world. It appears that these men were to be the spiritual caretakers of the body. The deacons (servants), on the other hand, were to deal with the day to day practical affairs of the church. They also were to be worthy of respect. If the church was to become strong and continue to grow it was imperative that its leadership be above reproach and capable of standing against the persecution of the world.

PAUL'S LAST LETTER

2 TIMOTHY

KEY WORD: PAUL'S FAREWELL

The historical setting has changed for Paul's second letter to Timothy. His first letter had been written after he had been released from his Roman imprisonment, so he was a free man. But a few years later he was again arrested, this time as a criminal (2:9). It is quite possible that Nero, the emperor, was looking for a scapegoat in regards to the fire which he himself had set in Rome, so he chose the Christians. Who better to arrest than Paul, their leader?

His trial had proceeded far enough that he knew there was no hope of escape. While waiting in the Roman prison for his "departure" (4:6), he wrote this second letter to Timothy, his son in the faith, and trusted coworker. His main themes are: 1) his own example, 2) endurance, 3) the power of scripture, and 4) his personal exhortations to Timothy.

PAUL'S EXAMPLE

Paul tells Timothy, "You know all about my teaching, my way of life, my purpose, faith, patience, love, endurance, persecutions, sufferings what kinds of things happened to me . . . , the persecutions I endured" (3:10,11). "Join with me in suffering for the Gospel" (1:8). Paul also speaks all throughout the book of his personal persecutions, and how the Lord continually delivered him (if not physically, then spiritually and emotionally). What an example he was leaving for a young minister who seemed to have great potential, but who also appeared to possess a spirit of timidity (1:7).

ENDURANCE

Paul relates Christianity and endurance to six common things in life, each of which must persevere. Soldiers, athletes, farmers, workmen, instruments, and servants must all endure if they expect to receive their reward. So it is true with a Christian, especially a Christian minister.

THE POWER OF SCRIPTURE

Paul knows that he will be gone soon, and that Timothy will not be able to depend on Paul for support and courage. So . . . he lets him know what truly changes lives. He says that "all scripture is God-breathed and is useful for teaching, rebuking, correcting, and training in righteousness, so that the man of God may be thoroughly equipped for every good work" (3:16, 17). It makes people wise unto salvation (3:15). It must be preached in season and out (4:2). And it must be multiplied through other faithful men (2:2).

PERSONAL EXHORTATIONS TO TIMOTHY

In a very serious way, Paul exhorts Timothy to more courage and Christian vitality. He tells him to: fan into flame the gift of God (1:6), be less timid (1:7), not be ashamed to testify about the Lord (1:8), guard the good deposit entrusted to him (1:14), be strong (2:1), endure hardship (2:3), flee evil desires of youth (2:22), preach the word (4:2), do the work of an evangelist (4:5), and to discharge all the duties of his ministry (4:5).

Second Timothy is a solemn letter. Its seriousness can be heard in every word. Yet in spite of this, Paul wishes to communicate victory!! He says "I have fought the good fight, I have finished the race, I have kept the faith. Now there is in store for me the crown of righteousness, which the Lord, the righteous judge, will award to me on that day" (4:7,8).

PAUL'S ADVICE TO THE MINISTER AT CRETE

TITUS

KEY WORD: SOUND DOCTRINE LEADING TO GOOD WORKS

Although we never see Titus mentioned in the book of Acts, he was one of Paul's closest and most trusted companions when it came to establishing churches. After being released from his first Roman imprisonment, Paul returned east, and as he went through Crete, he left Titus behind to "straighten out what was left unfinished" (1:5).

Crete is a mountainous island about 156 miles long and up to 35 miles wide, lying at the southern end of the Aegean Sea. Inhabitants from Crete were known to be wicked, lazy, and dishonest (1:12,13). A number of Jews from Crete were present in Jerusalem at the Day of Pentecost (Acts 2:11), which most likely resulted in churches being established throughout the island.

So . . . Paul writes to strengthen his co-worker. He develops three themes throughout the letter, 1) church leaders, 2) sound doctrine, and 3) good works.

CHURCH LEADERS

After Paul's greeting he sets out to help Titus to "straighten out what was left unfinished" (1:5). The first step was for Titus to appoint elders (overseers) in every town. These church leaders were to be blameless in three specific areas. They were to be: 1) in control of their homes, 2) in control of their own character, and 3) under the control of sound Biblical doctrine.

SOUND DOCTRINE

This is to be the base for everything that is done on the local church level. It was the only true way to silence the false teachers (1:9-11). It was to be taught with integrity so that their opponents would have nothing bad to say about them (2:7-8). It was to be obeyed, so that others would be attracted to it (2:10). Paul relates this "sound doctrine" to older men, older women, young men, and slaves, and in each case exhorts these people to live lives bringing glory to the heavenly Father (2:1-10).

Paul also instructs Titus to stress the proper teachings because it led to good works (3:8).

GOOD WORKS

Six times Paul mentions the concept of good works. 1) The false teachers were "unfit for doing anything good" (1:16). 2) Titus was to be an example to the Cretan believers by "doing what is good" (2:7). 3) God's people are "eager to do what is good" (2:14). 4) The people were "to do whatever is good" (3:1). 5) Those who trust in God should "be careful to devote themselves to doing what is good" (3:8). And 6) Paul simply confides in Titus that "our people must learn to devote themselves to doing what is good" (3:14).

A SLAVE BECOMES A BROTHER

PHILEMON

KEY WORD: FORGIVENESS

Philemon was a Christian residing in Colossae. Philemon's house was large enough to serve as the meeting place there, which suggests a degree of wealth. Paul seems to know Philemon and his character well as he writes this small letter to him.

While a prisoner in Rome, Paul came in contact with Philemon's runaway slave, Onesimus, and led him to the Lord (v. 10). It appears that he had robbed or in some way wronged his master, and then escaped. Paul grew to be close to Onesimus, and called him "my son" (v. 10), "my very heart" (v. 12), and "a dear brother" (v. 16). He wanted the slave to stay with him, but realized that he must be sent back to his master in order to set things right.

So . . . Paul sends Onesimus back to Philemon with this small letter in his hands. He appealed to Philemon to accept him "no longer as a slave, but better than a slave, as a dear brother" (v. 16).

As Paul appeals to Philemon to forgive and receive his repentant slave, he reminds him that Philemon owes Paul his very life (v. 19).

Philemon is not a direct attack on the institution of slavery, but its Christian principles would ultimately lead to the renunciation of slavery.

SERMONS TO JEWISH CHRISTIANS
HEBREWS
KEY WORD: BETTER

This is the only New Testament book whose background is surrounded in uncertainty. Who wrote it, where was it written, to whom was it written and when was it written?

Much speculation has gone into many theories concerning the author of this letter. Some say Paul, others Barnabas, Luke, Clement, Apollos, Silas, Philip, and even Priscilla. We can be certain, along with the third century theologian Origen that, "Who it was that really wrote the epistle, God only knows."

Concerning the other issues of uncertainty, we can only be sure that the letter was written to a group of Jewish Christians (even the title suggests this). It appears that these people may have been returning to their roots in Judaism, as the writer makes many contrasts between Christianity and Judaism.

The key word is "better", occurring thirteen times throughout the book. The writer is simply trying to show that the new covenant in Christ is so much better and superior than the old covenant of the law.

CHRIST: A BETTER PERSON — 1:1-4:13

Better than the *prophets* (l:l-3). Although God spoke through the prophets, Christ is heir of all things, creator of the universe, the radiance of God's glory, and the exact representation of God. After He redeemed mankind, He sat down at the right hand of God.

Better than *angels* (1:4-2:18). He is their creator. They worship Him. He is the Son, while they are servants. For a time (physical life on earth) He was "lower than the angels" but after His death He was "crowned with glory and honor".

Better than *Moses* (3:1-19). Moses was faithful as a servant in God's house, whereas Christ is faithful as a Son over God's house.

Better than *Joshua* (4:1-13). Joshua led the Israelites into the rest of the Promised Land. Christ leads believers into the rest of Heaven.

SO WHAT!?! The author does not teach these things without expecting it to change his hearers. Many letters contain a section of information followed with a section of application. This letter, however, has application throughout. When a point is brought home to the readers, it is then followed with thoughts of application.

The main thoughts of application in this section are warnings not to fall away:

— Pay more careful attention, so that we do not drift away (2:1).
— See to it that none of you has a sinful, unbelieving heart that turns away from the living God (3:12).
— Be careful that none of you be found to have fallen short of God's rest (4:1).
— Make every effort to enter that rest (4:11).

CHRIST'S A BETTER WORK — 4:14-10:18

Here begins the main theme of the book; that being a comparison of the old covenant of the "law" with the new covenant in "Christ".

OLD COVENANT OF "LAW"	NEW COVENANT IN "CHRIST"
– High Priest with no sympathy (4:15)	– Christ relates & sympathizes with our weaknesses (4:15)
– A High Priest among men (5:1)	– Great High Priest – Son of God (4:14)
– Like Aaron (7:11)	– Like Melchizedek (6:20-7:17)
– Weak and useless (7:18)	– Guarantee of better covenant (7:22)

- The priests died (7:23)
- Constant change (7:23)
- Priests were unable to save
- Sinful and imperfect Priests (7:27,28)
- They served in earthly sanctuary (8:5)
- Obsolete and aging covenant (8:13)
- Laws written on stone (9:4)
- No conscience clearing (9:9)
- Yearly sacrifice for sin (9:25)
- Sacrifices took away no sins (10:11)
- Offered the blood of bulls and goats (10:4)

- Jesus lives forever (7:24)
- Permanent Priesthood (7:24)
- Able to save completely (7:25)
- Sinless and perfect (7:26,28)
- Serves in heaven (8:1)
- Mediator of a better covenant (8:5)
- Laws written on hearts (8:10)
- Obtained eternal redemption (9:12)
- One sacrifice for sin (9:28)
- Brought holiness and perfection to believers (10:10,14)
- Offered Himself voluntarily (10:12)

What Christ offers is so much better than the Law!

In this section also there is straightforward application. The author tells his readers to leave the elementary teachings about Christ and go on to maturity (6:1). It seems that they had allowed Judaism to pull them backwards in their walk with God instead of allowing Christ to push them forwards. They are also reminded of the possibility that they could fall away (6:4-6), but it is followed by an encouraging section regarding the faithfulness of God and His promises (6:9-20).

CHRISTIANITY: A BETTER WALK — 10:19-13:25

The author now applies what he has said to the faith of his readers. Since Christ and His new covenant are superior, then we must draw near to God, keep our hope, spur one another on toward love and good deeds, realize that it is a dreadful thing to fall into the hands of the living God, and persevere (10:19-39).

The faith that the readers must maintain is defined in chapter 11, verses 1-3, and illustrated in verses 4-40. By relating their lives to these great Old Testament heroes, they were to have more faith, perseverance and hope in what God had promised.

Next Christ's example of enduring hardship is given to Christians (12:1-13). We should endure hardship as discipline, expecting a harvest of righteousness as a result.

He then goes on to relate the old covenant of fear (12:18-21) to the new covenant of blessings (12:22-24). With these blessings coming, we must humbly accept them and worship God acceptably with reverance and awe, for our God is a consuming fire (12:25-29).

Chapter 13 gives us the author's concluding instructions for mature Christian living. He then closes with a beautiful benediction and some personal words.

THE NEW TESTAMENT BOOK OF PROVERBS

JAMES

KEY WORD: FAITH: DEAD OR ALIVE?

James was a half-brother of the Lord Jesus who at this time in history was a leader in the church at Jerusalem. However, once he had disbelieved the claims of Jesus (John 7:5). But after the risen Lord appeared to him (1 Corinthians 9:5), he was thoroughly convinced. He was known as a good man and was given the title "The Just" by his countrymen. It is said that he spent so much time on his knees in prayer that they became hard and calloused like a camel's knees.

He wrote this letter to the "twelve tribes scattered among the nations" (1:1). These Jewish Christians were being persecuted in many ways, and James wanted to encourage them to continue to live out their faith.

The key word is: "Faith: Dead or Alive?" James wanted his readers to seriously evaluate their faith in Christ. Was it a mere acceptance of and belief in true doctrine? Was it a verbal and mental faith? James would call this faith "dead faith". Or did these people have faith that led to action? Real faith would be evidenced in a life through the person's conduct and character.

While doctrinal truths underlie James' comments, his purpose is not doctrinal, but practical. This letter is so practical that it has been called the "New Testament Book of proverbs". Like "Proverbs" it shifts quickly from topic to topic. Let's take a look.

TRIALS	– Consider it joy, because they develop maturity (1:2-4).
PRAYERS OF FAITH	– Don't doubt, or prayers won't be answered (1:5-8).
RICHES	– Don't depend on them, for like a plant they can wither (1:9-11).
TEMPTATION	– God does not tempt – our evil desires tempt us. If we give in, it leads to death (1:12-15).

BLESSINGS	**–Come from God, Who does not change (1:16-18).**
ANGER	**–Does not lead to righteousness (1:19-21).**
THE WORD	**–Do it! = Blessings (1:22-25).**
PURE RELIGION	**–Caring for those in need and not becoming polluted by the world (1:26-27).**
FAVORITISM	**–Don't! Aren't the rich exploiting you, and the poor inheriting the kingdom? Mercy triumphs over judgment (2:1-13).**
FAITH AND WORKS	**–Cannot be separated. They are both sides of the same coin. Faith without works is dead (2:14-26).**
THE TONGUE	**–Should reflect the inner character of Christlikeness (3:1-12).**
WISDOM	**–Is simply being smart enough to do that which is right (3:13-18).**
QUARRELS	**–Come from selfish covetousness (4:1,2).**
UNANSWERED PRAYER	**–Happens when we're selfish (4:3).**
WORLDLINESS	**–Shows hatred of God. Instead submit, resist the devil, come near to God, and be humble (4:4-10).**
JUDGING	**–Don't, because God is the only Judge (4:11,12).**
THE LORD'S WILL	**–Don't assume that your plans are God's (4:13-17).**
RICHES	**–Here James put the fear of God in those who were rich (5:1-6).**
PATIENCE	**–Endure hardship, knowing that rewards will be great (5:7-11).**
SWEARING	**–Don't! Simply do what you say you'll do (5:12).**
PRAYER	**–Of a righteous man is powerful and effective (5:13).**
TURNING A BROTHER BACK TO GOD	**–Will cover over a multitude of sins (5:19,20).**

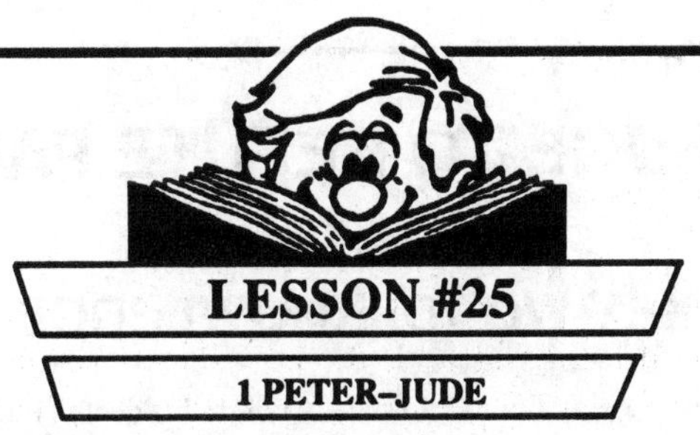

THE NEW TESTAMENT BOOK OF "JOB"

1 PETER

KEY WORD: HOPE IN SUFFERING

Peter was one of the original twelve apostles. While Christ was still on earth Peter's life seemed to be a roller-coaster. His emotions and actions fluctuated, so that at one point he boldly stated that Jesus was the Christ, and at another point he denied Christ three times. But, Peter's life was dramatically changed after Christ's resurrection and ascension. He occupied a central role in the early church and in the spread of the gospel to the Samaritans and Gentiles (Acts 2-10). After the Jerusalem Council in Acts 15, little is recorded of Peter's activities. He evidently traveled extensively with his wife (1 Cor. 9:5) and ministered in various Roman provinces. According to tradition, Peter was crucified upside down in Rome prior to Nero's death in A.D. 68.

He wrote this letter in response to the growing opposition to the believers, both Jewish and Gentile, in Asia Minor. The Roman emperor, Nero, was severely persecuting the believers in and around Rome. It had literally become a "painful trial" (4:12), as Christians were being burned in Nero's gardens, and were also being fed to the lions in his arena. This gave an example to others throughout the Roman world to also persecute Christians. So . . . Peter wrote this letter to give hope in the midst of suffering.

BLESSINGS IN CHRIST — 1:1-2:12

The best way for anyone to handle suffering is to have faith in the proper things. Instead of addressing the issue of suffering from the beginning, Peter begins with the basics of the faith. If these people would rely on these basic foundational truths, then the suffering would be easier to endure. All throughout this section, then, we see God's grace and mercy which has resulted in our many blessings in Christ.

Peter writes, "praise be to the God and Father of our Lord Jesus Christ! In His great *mercy* He has given us *new birth* into a *living hope through the resurrection of Jesus Christ from the dead*, and into an *inheritance* that can *never perish*, spoil or fade, kept *in heaven for you*, who through faith are *shielded by God's power* until the coming of the *salvation* that is ready to be revealed in the last time" (1:3-5). He continues by telling them that their sufferings would prove their faith genuine, which would result in praise, glory and honor when Jesus Christ is revealed (1:7). He also tells them that they were a "chosen people, a royal priesthood, a holy nation, a people belonging to God" (2:9), and that they were "aliens and strangers in this world" (2:11). His purpose throughout this section is to get their eyes off of themselves, and onto Christ and what He has done for them and made them to become. He realizes that to truly change someone, you must change their way of thinking.

SUBMISSION IN CHRIST — 2:13-3:12

Suffering was coming from all sides; from the king, governors, masters, husbands, etc. The Christian's response is to submit to those who have authority over them. In this way by doing good they can silence the ignorant talk of foolish men. And in so doing, they should look to Christ, Who, when persecuted, made no threats of retaliation, but simply entrusted Himself to God.

SUFFERING IN CHRIST — 3:13-5:14

Peter points out clearly that trials and suffering are not strange things to experience as Christians. But he also clearly states that the sufferings should come as a result of our Christian lifestyle, not sinful behavior (3:17; 4:15,16). The Christian should rejoice that they have shared in Christ's sufferings, knowing that they will also share in His glory.

Throughout the book Peter also gives many guidelines for Christian living; things such as humility, self-control, hospitality, etc. But he says "above all, love each other deeply, because love covers over a multitude of sins" (4:8).

USING KNOWLEDGE TO REFUTE FALSE TEACHING

2 PETER

KEY WORD: KNOWLEDGE

The apostle Peter wrote this second letter to Asia Minor (3:1) shortly before his death (1:13-15), within a few years after 1 Peter was written. In 1 Peter he addressed the issue of persecution from the outside; he now writes about problems from within. He warns his readers about false teachers and tells them that a knowledge of the truth is their best defense against this attack from within the church.

THE IMPORTANCE OF KNOWLEDGE — CHAPTER 1

The best defense for error is a proper, mature understanding of truth; not simply a mental belief, but a life-changing faith and knowledge. This knowledge taps us into God's power, which can meet all of our needs (1:3). It also demands that we grow in faith, goodness, self-control, perseverance, godliness, brotherly kindness, and love (1:5-7). This knowledge has been given by eyewitnesses (1:16), and through God's prophets (1:19), who spoke from God as they were led by the Holy Spirit (1:21).

In this section Peter also lets his friends know of his impending death, comparing his body to a tent which must be put aside (1:13-15).

FALSE TEACHERS: THEIR MOTIVATION, SCHEMES, AND DESTRUCTION - CHAPTER 2

Peter's discussion of true prophecy (1:19-21) leads him to denounce the false prophecy in the churches. The false teachers' motivation is greed (2:3) and arrogance (2:10). Their schemes would include: secretly introducing destructive heresies (2:1), exploiting with their own stories (2:3), slandering celestial beings (2:10), appealing to lustful desires (2:18), enticing new believers (2:18), and promising freedom (2:19). But, they are like brute beasts who will perish (2:12), and who have blackest darkness reserved for them (2:17). If God did not spare angels who sinned (2:4), or the ancient world when they sinned (2:5), or Sodom and Gomorrah in their sin (2:6), then He will certainly judge and punish these men (2:9). Notice that this entire chapter is not speaking against the world, but against some in the church.

THE LORD'S SECOND COMING — CHAPTER 3

The false teachers also pervert the truth of Christ's second coming (3:3,4). But the Lord will come (3:10), even though we know not when (3:8, 9). And it will be a day of destruction for the ungodly (3:7), and of reward for the godly (3:13). Therefore, Christians should live holy and godly lives (3:11), and make every effort to be found spotless, blameless, and at peace with God (3:14).

KNOWLEDGE LEADS TO OBEDIENCE & FELLOWSHIP

1 JOHN

KEY WORD: WALK THE WALK

According to early church tradition, the apostle John made his home in Ephesus after the destruction of Jerusalem in 70 A.D. Here John lived to an old age, at which he began to write his gospel and letters. His writings are at least ten years after any of the other New Testament books, so they give us a different perspective on the church, and the world. Although there is no address, it is likely that 1 John was written to the Asian churches that were within the realm of his oversight at Ephesus.

1 John seems to serve two purposes: l) a positive encouragement to an obedient walk in Christ, and 2) a negative attack against the false teachings of Gnosticism. Remember that in Gnosticism the flesh was considered totally evil, so John wants to vividly show Christ's humanity (His physical, fleshly nature, but to have self-control in regards to His body.)

This letter is difficult to outline, because John intertwines his themes and topics. The following has been given as a simple outline to the letter.

FELLOWSHIP WITH GOD — 1:1-2:2

John begins with thoughts concerning Christ's physicalness. They had heard, seen, and touched Jesus. He was the "Word of Life."

John's purpose for the letter was to get people in fellowship with God (1:3) by walking in light (1:5-7) and repenting of sins (1:8-10). This fellowship comes through the atoning sacrifice of Jesus (2:1,2).

WALK AS JESUS WALKED — 2:3-27

The focus to this section is Christian obedience. If we want to be "in Christ" we must "walk as Jesus did" (2:6). Practically speaking this is obeying His commands (2:3-5), and not giving in to the pressures of this world (2:15-17).

In this section John also mentions the anti-Christ, who would come before Christ's second coming. This is the same person referred to in 2 Thessalonians, according to many commentators.

CONTINUE IN HIM — 2:28-3:10

By continuing in Christ we will not be ashamed at His second coming (2:28). We are born of God and are now His children (2:29-3:1). We've been made pure (3:3) and righteous (3:7).

LOVE ONE ANOTHER — 3:11-5:4A

The word "love" is used 39 times in this section. What is love? Simply this, "God is love" (4:8) and He sent Jesus to lay down His life for us (3:16), so that we would love one another (3:23). This love is not simply a heart felt emotion. It is action! (3:18). It springs forth in our life because of our great love for God.

FAITH — 5:4B-21

Our faith brings the victory in overcoming the world (5:4). It also brings the confidence and assurance of eternal life (5:13), the realization that we are God's children (5:19), and the commitment not to sin (5:18).

WARNING ABOUT FALSE TEACHERS

2 JOHN

KEY WORD: WATCH OUT

2 John is a brief note to either a prominent woman in a local church, or simply a specific local church ("chosen lady" taken symbolically as referring to a specific church), to whom he wished to visit soon. John begins by referring to the "truth" of God five times in the first four verses. This "truth" was the basis of life "in Christ", and led John to repeat what he considers to be "*THE*" command of Christ: "Loving one another."

John turns from his positive thoughts of truth and love to his negative warning to the "chosen lady" concerning false teachers. John seems to here be concerned with one major false doctrine — that being the teaching that Christ did not come in the flesh. This, again, comes from Gnostic thinking. John's advice is to never allow anyone like this to enter a Christian's home, which would be a way of sharing in his wicked work.

CONTRASTING GOOD & BAD CHURCH LEADERS

3 JOHN

KEY WORD: CONTRASTING LEADERS

This is a brief note (3 John is the shortest book in the Bible) from John to a beloved church leader, Gaius.

It seems that John had sent out some traveling preachers to encourage the churches. This letter simply contrasts the response of two church leaders to these preachers. Gaius warmly accepts them with hospitality, and receives a commendation from John. Diotrephes, on the other hand, rejects the preachers, gossips about the work of John, and would even excommunicate anyone in his church who accepted the preachers. The stark reality of the message in this letter is that many church leaders in our churches today are like Diotrephes; wanting total control and showing no love and trust in their brothers.

EXPOSING FALSE TEACHERS
JUDE
KEY WORD: FALSE TEACHERS

Jude was a half-brother of Jesus, who, like his brother James, did not believe the claims of Jesus until after the resurrection. Very little is known about him. This letter is very similar to 2 Peter (especially chapter 2), and scholars believe that Jude used Peter's letter as a source for writing his own letter.

He says that he wanted to write to them about the general theme of "salvation", but their problem with false teachers prompted him to strongly attack this problem. Jude focuses more on the false teachers than on their teachings. He says that they are godless men, dreamers, unreasoning animals, and shepherds who feed only themselves. He relates them to the Old Testament references of: l) disbelieving Israelites, 2) angels who abandoned their home, 3) Sodom and Gomorrah, 4) Cain, 5) Balaam, and 6) Korah, who all received their due punishment in time. They reject authority, pollute their bodies, speak abusively about things they don't understand, grumble, boast about themselves, and continually find fault in others.

In contrast to the false teachers that are self-pleasing, and have not the Spirit, Christians are to build themselves up, pray in the Spirit, keep themselves in the love of God, and look for the mercy of the Lord.

THE FINAL ACT

REVELATION

KEY WORD: VICTORY IN JESUS!

This book is likely the most neglected book of the New Testament. This is simply due to the fact that the book abounds in visions, symbols, and veiled expressions. Yet the title of the book suggests just the opposite of neglect, as it states that the book is the "revelation of Jesus Christ". It is therefore a "revealing", an "uncovering" of things which were about to take place.

Scholars cannot agree on the meaning of many of the images in the book (perhaps this also is why people fear it, and therefore ignore it). It is therefore important to keep an open, humble mind as we come to the book, realizing that we may not have an answer to each question that arises. But, we can understand the simple message of the book. This lesson, therefore, seeks not to discuss the myriads of theories, but to present the theme and focus of the book in simple form, that being: "*VICTORY IN JESUS*." Much of the material for this lesson was taken from William Hendricksen's book, *More Than Conquerors.*

"Revelation" was written by the apostle John while he was an exile on the island of Patmos (1:9,) in approximately 96 A.D. It was originally sent to the "seven churches of Asia" (1:4). To have a sound interpretation of the book, one must continually remember the context in which it was written. The church was now over 60 years old. For the first 30 years she basically operated unmolested by imperial Rome. Then things changed. The First Imperial Persecution of Christians took place from 64-67 A.D. under Nero. It was during this persecution that both Peter and Paul suffered martyrdom. The Second Imperial Persecution was instituted by Emperor Domitian, 95-96 A.D. Over 40,000 Christians were severely tortured and slain. This was the persecution in which John was banished to the Isle of Patmos. The Third Imperial Persecution, that of Trajan, was soon to begin, 98 A.D. John had lived through the first two and was about to enter the third. The "Revelation" was given to inspire the Christians to remain steadfast even under the most severe conditions knowing that regardless of what might happen, they would have *VICTORY IN JESUS*!

VICTORY IN JESUS! This is the simple theme of the book of Revelation. Persecuted believers down through the ages could turn to the pages of this book for comfort and hope. No matter how bad things might seem, "Revelation" makes us see the reality that Christ lives and reigns, and someday He will totally destroy Satan and take the Christians to heaven to live eternally with Him.

INTRODUCTION — CHAPTER 1

The revelation was received by Christ from the Father and communicated by an angel to John (1:1,2). It is the only book that promises a blessing to those who read it (1:3). Likewise, a curse is given to those who add to or take away from it (22:18,19). It was written to the seven churches of Asia Minor (1:11).

LETTERS TO SEVEN CHURCHES — CHAPTERS 2 & 3

Before revealing things to come at later times, Jesus chooses to send letters to 7 of the churches (called lampstands because churches everywhere are to shine forth the gospel into the darkness of this world) of the day. *Ephesus* had worked hard, refused to tolerate wicked men, endured hardship, but still had lost its first love. *Smyrna* receives encouragement to endure suffering. *Pergamum* has remained true to Christ's name, yet has tolerated immorality. *Thyatira* receives praise for her deeds, yet has tolerated an evil woman. *Sardis* is condemned for being dead. *Philadelphia* has endured patiently, and is reminded of Christ's soon coming. *Laodicea* is lukewarm and in danger of being rejected by Christ.

Each of these letters must first be seen in the context of the first century church. Then, we can see these letters as warnings for future congregations. What local body of believers cannot apply these letters to their situation? None! Therefore, "he who has an ear" (reads and understands these letters), "let him hear" (do it!).

THE SEALS OF PERSECUTION — CHAPTERS 4-7

In this passage revelations of future events (for John) begin to take place, and continue throughout the book.

The scene opens describing the One who sits on the throne receiving worship from those who surround Him. He holds a scroll which no one is found worthy to unseal, except the Lamb of God. As He opens the first of seven seals, we see Christ on a white horse. As He opens the next 3 seals we see persecution upon Christ's saints; war, famine, and death. This represents that throughout the life of the church the world would persecute the church in every conceivable way. The fifth seal reveals "under the altar the souls of those who had been slain because of the word of God and the testimony they had maintained" (6:9). These represent those persecuted under the 2nd, 3rd, and 4th seals. They are crying out for vengeance. The sixth seal being opened revealed catastrophic events associated with Judgment Day. The opening of the 7th seal revealed seven trumpets.

This first set of visions, as with the two that will follow (trumpets and bowls), covers the entire Christian era (from Christ's first coming through His second coming).

THE TRUMPETS OF WARNING — CHAPTERS 8-14

Following the seals of persecution the Lord sends forth His trumpets of warning. They do not represent single events, but they rather refer to terrible calamities that will occur again and again throughout the Christian era. — calamities which are sent upon the wicked in order to punish them and warn them concerning their opposition of Christ and His people. These are not God's final judgment, but rather a warning of that coming event. Yet, in spite of all these warnings, mankind in general does not repent (9:20). This lack of repentance would one day cause God to bring forth His bowls of wrath.

Also in this section we are taken back to the manger scene of the Christ-child (12:1-17). When it seemed that Satan could not defeat the Christ, he attacked Christ's saints, the church. But this passage also ends with words of comfort for afflicted Christians. Anyone who followed the dragon or his helpers was doomed for God's wrath.

THE BOWLS OF WRATH — CHAPTERS 15-19

Now what will God do to those who have persecuted His righteous saints, and have not heeded the trumpet warnings to repent? This passage speaks to this issue. Whenever in history the wicked fail to repent, the natural result will be God's wrath. His wrath is then considered "final" for these individuals, because there is no opportunity for repentance hereafter. So . . . all throughout the Christian era the horror of God's wrath has been poured out on those who would not respond to Him. Finally, one day, the Day of Judgment, these people will receive their final measure of God's wrath. This section also describes the seductions of this world (Babylon), and the destruction thereof. The destruction of the beast and the false prophet (Satan's helpers) is also mentioned.

THE FINAL ACT — CHAPTERS 20-22

THIS IS IT! All of biblical history leads up to this one event: JUDGMENT DAY! This is where Satan is finally thrown into the lake of burning sulfur, where he will be tormented day and night forever and ever (20:10). He will be joined by all those whose names were not found in the Book of Life.

But for those who overcame the schemes of Satan, God has prepared a "New Jerusalem" with splendor beyond comprehension. A place where there is no death, mourning, crying, or pain. A place where the sun is not needed, for the glory of the Lord gives it light.

The book closes with Christ's promise "I am coming soon" and with the response of His people who say, "COME!"

Think again about what this book meant to the Christians of John's day who were enduring the persecutions of the emperor, Domitian. It helps them to see that they still have the responsibility of being light-bearers in their communities (the 7 letters to the churches — chapters 2 & 3). It also helps them to realize that persecutions will come upon Christians (the 7 seals of persecution — chapters 4-7). But, God will not leave the persecutors unpunished (the 7 trumpets of warning — chapters 8-14), and will one day pour out His bowls of wrath as His final and total retribution (chapters 15-19). As the pagan world is thrown into the lake of burning sulfur, the Christians are ushered into their New Jerusalem for their wedding feast with the Lamb (chapters 20-22).

What *hope* this message gives to Christians of any age. Things are not always as they seem. Satan cannot win! *JESUS IS THE VICTOR, THE CONQUEROR!* He is victorious, therefore, so are we! PRAISE HIS NAME!!!

As Genesis was the book of "beginnings", so Revelation is the book of completion. Genesis introduced us to many things which see their fulfillment in Revelation. Let's take a look:

Genesis	Revelation
1) God created heavens and earth (1:1)	New heaven and earth (21:1)
2) Darkness called "night" (1:5)	No more night (22:5)
3) Gathered waters called "seas" (1:10)	No more seas (21:1)
4) Sun and moon created (1:16)	God is the Light (21:23)
5) Satan appears (3:1)	Satan disappears (20:10)
6) Sin is introduced (3:1-13)	Sin is gone (21:27)
7) Man fleeing from God (3:8)	Dwelling with God (21:3)
8) Satan is cursed (3:14)	Satan is destroyed (20:10)
9) Pain increased (3:16)	No more pain (21:4)
10) Ground is cursed (3:17)	No more curse (22:3)
11) Death introduced (3:19)	No more death (21:4)
12) Paradise lost (3:23)	Paradise restored (21:10-21)
13) Access to tree of life cut off (3:24)	Tree of life re-appears (22:2)
14) Driven from God (3:24)	Living with God (21:3)

MY PERSONAL DAILY BIBLE STUDY

Why do we study the Bible?

Paul prays a prayer in the book of Colossians which states the purpose of Bible Study:

> "For this reason, since the day we heard about you, we have not stopped praying for you and asking God to fill you with the knowledge of His will through all spiritual wisdom and understanding. And we pray this in order that you may live a life worthy of the Lord and may please Him in every way: Bearing fruit in every good work, growing in the knowledge of God." Colossians 1:9, 10

Paul prays that God would "Fill us with the knowledge of His will." But notice that this knowledge is not the goal in and of itself. Paul goes on to say "In order that," or, "For the purpose of," "Living a life worthy of the Lord."

Notice that our Bible study should never be for the purpose of acquiring knowledge only, but for helping us in the process of "living a life worthy of the Lord."

God's word is really a mirror for our spiritual lives — to show us where we need to change in order to **"live a life** worthy of the Lord."

"Do not merely listen to the word, and so deceive yourselves. Do what it says. Anyone who listens to the word but does not do what it says is like a man who looks at his face in a mirror and, after looking at himself, goes away and immediately forgets what he looks like. But the man who looks intently into the perfect law that gives freedom, and continues to do this, not forgetting what he has heard, but doing it — he will be blessed in what he does." James 1:22-25

In striving to live a "life worthy of the Lord," the Bible then becomes an invaluable tool for pointing out to us where we need to change.

As children of the King we need to continually be growing and changing to become the people that God wants us to become. The Bible therefore becomes the "Change-Agent," stimulating us in this growth process.

Each of us needs his/her own personal daily Bible study time, just as we need a daily prayer time. This will ensure that our walk with our Lord will always stay alive, and not become stagnant.

Let's not just talk about its importance. Let's talk practically about "How To" study the Bible. There are certain variables that need to be thought through. Things such as:

TIME

You will never "find" time to really study the Bible — you have to "make" time!!! You're a busy person. You'll need to arrange for a study time, plan on it, hold to it, and don't let things interrupt. Select a time when you are physically and mentally alert, and resolve to stick to it.

My best time to study my Bible would be ______________________________.

PLACE

Important considerations are: the room, the desk, the chair, the lighting, an atmosphere that aids concentration, and privacy to prevent distractions.

My best place to study my Bible would be ______________________________.

BIBLE

This is sooooooo important. #1) Don't use a Paraphrase. In a Paraphrase the writers take a thought from the original language and change it into English, whereas, in a translation, the writers translate each word into its English equivalent. Quite often in a Paraphrase something is left out that God wants left in.

#2) Don't use a one-man translation. Quite often this man will have biases that will come out in his translation.

#3) Find a group effort translation that you feel comfortable with. The New American Standard Version, Revised Standard Version, New International Version, and New King James Version are all excellent.

#4) Mark in your Bible. As you are reading, and something seems especially important — underline it. Write down cross references, jot down special points made in sermons or lessons, record any insights that you might have. Do whatever you need to do to make your Bible a part of you, not just another book you happen to be studying.

TOOLS

There are many tools available to help us understand our Bibles better. Although they are not essential (the Bible is the only essential book), they are often helpful. Here's a list of possible tools: a Bible concordance, a Bible dictionary, a Bible handbook, Bible maps and atlases, and Bible commentaries.

METHODS

There are many very helpful methods available for learning Scripture better. Here is one method that will help immeasurably.

—**Pray.** Ask God to really help you concentrate on what He would want you to learn. Also, ask Him to soften your heart to the point where you would be willing to make any changes that He would ask you to make.

—**Read** through the passage a couple of times. Now put the main idea of the passage into title form (the shorter, the better). Now look back through the passage and decide what it is saying to you, and what you need to do (and possibly change) because of this passage.

—**Jot Down** any special insights you may have gained from the passage. You may want to ask yourself questions such as the following to aid in the discovery process.

—What does the passage mean to me?
—Are there any promises to claim?
—Are there commands to follow?
—Are there sins to avoid, or confess?
—Are there examples to follow?
—What will I do because of what I learned from this passage?

—**Pray.** After spending time in Bible study you should have much to talk to God about. You may praise Him for His greatness, thank Him for insights gained, confess sins, pray for others that came to mind during your study, or simply ask Him to help you to live according to what you've learned in His Word.

The following pages have been provided for you to make notes on your daily studies.
Permission is granted to copy the following two pages.

MY PERSONAL DAILY BIBLE STUDY

FOR THE WEEK OF __________ TO __________

SUNDAY DATE __________________ PASSAGE ______________________________

1) TITLE: (In your own words) ______________________________

2) WHAT DOES THIS PASSAGE MEAN FOR ME? WHAT WILL I DO (CHANGE) AS A RESULT OF THIS STUDY?______________________________

____

____

3) INSIGHTS:______________________________

____

MONDAY DATE __________________ PASSAGE ______________________________

1) TITLE: (In your own words) ______________________________

2) WHAT DOES THIS PASSAGE MEAN FOR ME? WHAT WILL I DO (CHANGE) AS A RESULT OF THIS STUDY?______________________________

____

____

3) INSIGHTS:______________________________

____

TUESDAY DATE __________________ PASSAGE ______________________________

1) TITLE: (In your own words) ______________________________

2) WHAT DOES THIS PASSAGE MEAN FOR ME? WHAT WILL I DO (CHANGE) AS A RESULT OF THIS STUDY?______________________________

____

____

3) INSIGHTS:______________________________

____

WEDNESDAY DATE ______ PASSAGE ______

1) TITLE: (In your own words) ______

2) WHAT DOES THIS PASSAGE MEAN FOR ME? WHAT WILL I DO (CHANGE) AS A RESULT OF THIS STUDY? ______

3) INSIGHTS: ______

THURSDAY DATE ______ PASSAGE ______

1) TITLE: (In your own words) ______

2) WHAT DOES THIS PASSAGE MEAN FOR ME? WHAT WILL I DO (CHANGE) AS A RESULT OF THIS STUDY? ______

3) INSIGHTS: ______

FRIDAY DATE ______ PASSAGE ______

1) TITLE: (In your own words) ______

2) WHAT DOES THIS PASSAGE MEAN FOR ME? WHAT WILL I DO (CHANGE) AS A RESULT OF THIS STUDY? ______

3) INSIGHTS: ______

SATURDAY DATE ______ PASSAGE ______

1) TITLE: (In your own words) ______

2) WHAT DOES THIS PASSAGE MEAN FOR ME? WHAT WILL I DO (CHANGE) AS A RESULT OF THIS STUDY? ______

3) INSIGHTS: ______

MY PERSONAL DAILY PRAYER TIME

In Luke 18:1-8 Jesus is teaching his disciples (and us) about the importance of being persistent in prayer, so He informs us of what will take place if we don't continue to pray. Luke writes, "...they should always pray and not give up." In this, the New International Version, it sounds like Jesus wants us to not give up praying. Let's take a closer look. The New American Standard Version puts it this way, "...they ought to pray and not to lose heart." And the King James Version says, "...ought always to pray, and not to faint." Another place in the New Testament this same Greek word is translated "collapse." So...what is Jesus trying to teach us? **He is teaching us that either we pray or we give up. Either we pray or we lose heart. Either we pray or we faint.**

Pray or Faint! There are no other options. Either we are a person of prayer, "casting our anxieties on Him," or we "lose heart," "give up," "faint." This is the importance of prayer: If we make prayer an important and regular part of our daily lives — we live the excited, radiant, abundant life that Jesus spoke of. If, however, we don't make prayer an important and regular part of our daily lives — we'll live a frustrated, discouraged, faint-hearted Christian life.

"Prayer is more than asking; prayer is taking. Prayer is more than pleading; prayer is believing. Prayer is more than words uttered; it is an attitude maintained. How many times we ought to be praying! Whenever there is an awareness of need, that is an opportunity to let the heart, the thought, and the voice (whatever form prayer may take) lift immediately to God and say, 'God, be merciful. Lord, meet this need. My hope, my help, my everything is in you for this moment.' It doesn't matter whether it is only tying your shoes or washing the dishes or writing a letter or turning out a paper or making a telephone call. Whenever there's need, that is the time for prayer. Prayer is that expression of dependence which lays hold of God's resources — for any need." [1] This is why Paul says, "pray continually," (1 Thessalonians 5:17), and "devote yourselves to prayer" (Colossians 4:2). Prayer is a continual sharing of our inadequacy with God's adequacy. This is one thing we must learn: there is no activity of life which does not require prayer, a sense of expectation of God at work.

HOW SHOULD I PRAY?

Although many people like to bow their heads and close their eyes (to show respect to God and to get rid of any possible distractions) when they pray — there is no "proper formula" in Scripture as to one's physical posture during prayer. Therefore, we will deal only with the mental and spiritual aspects of how we should pray — not the physical (however, let's not forget that a person's physical actions sometimes reflect the attitude of the heart — remember the parable in Luke 18:10-14).

IN FAITH

Believing beyond a shadow of a doubt that God hears and answers all of your prayers (James 1:5-8).

IN JESUS' NAME

By His authority, on the basis of His character, in the value of His work (John 14:13). It is the same concept as praying "according to God's will" as found in 1 John 5:14, 15. When we pray, we are only to pray within the scope of what Jesus would be proud of, or what He would pray if He were physically present.

GOD ALWAYS ANSWERS

When we pray, we know that God has answered our prayer. But sometimes we need to consider how God answers prayer. He either says "yes," "no," or "wait." So...if things aren't going quite as we thought they would, either God said "no," or He said "wait." Strong patience and faith in God are natural by-products of waiting on God. When God says "no" He is simply saying that He knows what is best for us. What we want is not always what we need. God gives us what we need. No matter what God's answer may be, we should "pray continually; giving thanks in all circumstances, for this is God's will for you in Christ Jesus" (1 Thessalonians 5:17, 18).

DIFFERENT ASPECTS OF PRAYER

Prayer needs to be a continual, on-going communion with the Father. In addition, however, each of us needs to have a time set aside each day for concentrated, directed, and unhurried prayer. Find a time when you can get away from the distractions of life and communicate with God. Following are five different aspects that this kind of prayer can take.

ADORATION

This is the aspect of prayer where we worship God, praise Him, revere Him, adore Him, and stand in awe before Him because of how much He has done for us. This is our opportunity in prayer to say in many ways, "God, I Love You!"

CONFESSION

Once we have lifted God up through our adoration of Him — we naturally see how inadequate and sinful we are. So...we confess our sins to Him and He "forgives us and purifies us from all unrighteousness" (1 John 1:9). This is admitting honestly and openly our sin against God, others, and ourselves, and repenting of each of these sins.

THANKSGIVING

When we realize that God has truly purified us — this leads us to a time of thanksgiving. We not only thank Him for forgiving us, but also for all the great things that He has done for us.

INTERCESSION

Just as prayers of adoration spring from love for God, prayers of intercession arise from love of men. This is our opportunity to pray for others. We should pray for: the lost, our friends, our enemies, our country, other nations, missionaries, our family, our church, our ministers, and our neighbors.

SUPPLICATION

Now comes the time to pray for yourself. "Cast all your anxiety on Him because He cares for you" (1 Peter 5:7). We should lift all of our needs up to the Father for His tender care. Our physical, spiritual, mental, and emotional needs will all be met if simply placed in the Father's hands.

USE A PRAYER LIST

Paul's epistles indicate not only an extensive prayer ministry for many, many people but many churches worldwide. To pray as consistently as he undoubtedly did would demand the systematic use of something akin to a prayer list. Yet a prayer list can lead to a shallow time of prayer, "God bless so and so." Therefore, only put specific prayer requests, things that need to be remembered daily, on your list. Then use it. Keep it up to date. Keep it accurate. The following pages are given so that you can begin your own systematic prayer time with God. Permission is granted to copy the Personal Prayer List.

Footnote:
1. Stedman, Ray, **"Jesus Teaches On Prayer"**, Word Books, Waco, Texas, 1975, p. 35.

PERSONAL PRAYER LIST

ADORATION — CONFESSION — THANKSGIVING — INTERCESSION — SUPPLICATION

PRAYER REQUEST	DATE	ANSWER

PERSONAL PRAYER LIST

ADORATION — CONFESSION — THANKSGIVING — INTERCESSION — SUPPLICATION

PRAYER REQUEST	DATE	ANSWER